MW00415265

ISBN-13: 978-1533159489

i

To Stephen, my co-author and best friend.

- Greg Foster

To Greg, the person who helped me write some of this and whom I occasionally talk to.

- Stephen Turban

TABLE OF CONTENTS

FOREWORD

When I first met Stephen Turban, I was struck by his instinct to ask the big questions and to make the most of his college years. He was a freshman at Harvard, and I was entering my ninth year as Dean of Freshmen. Subsequent conversations with him, and later with Greg Foster, convinced me that our office's initiative to create moments for reflection, with an emphasis on values and purpose, was sorely needed. So too was this book.

I used to think admiringly of colleagues who had what I considered the hard skills – the ability to be sharply analytical and to crunch impressive numbers. Then I came to see that those skills were not enough to be successful; it mattered to have emotional intelligence too. People who were good at active listening, putting themselves in someone else's shoes, being authentic, and being willing to devote the time to relationships were going to go far. They would surely know success.

When I think of success, I think not of climbing the proverbial professional ladder, perhaps with some degree of calculation, but of making a difference and finding personal fulfillment along the way. It has been interesting at my Harvard reunions to hear classmates talk of the importance of friendships begun in college and continued over the decades as people have been there for one another through the ups and downs of life. The same people would likely point to some great classes and

Your Relationship GPA

engaging activities as undergraduates, but they would put the relationships begun and nurtured as the centerpiece of their satisfaction. In my own experience, an annual "round table" organized with the same small group of classmates – over a long weekend consisting of heart-to-heart conversations, strengthened by the launching pad we shared in college fifty years ago – has been a key part of my feeling blessed.

I am so glad to see the topic of relationships taken up by Stephen and Greg, and think their message is a valuable one. Peers have a way of influencing peers. An early read will, no doubt, ensure a life of greater meaning and a life of fewer regrets.

- Thomas A. Dingman

Your Relationship GPA

1
INTRODUCTION

"Happiness is love. Full stop."

- George Vaillant, Director of the Grant Study

In 1938, Dr. Arlie Bock was fed up. By any standard, he had all the trappings of success: he was a professor at Harvard, he was the chief officer for student health, and his research involved strapping Olympic athletes to treadmills.[1] If that doesn't scream success, we're not sure what does.

And yet, Bock felt like his research was insignificant. He'd spent the past twenty years studying the chemical properties of blood; and though he'd become a renowned scholar in his field, he found himself unfulfilled. After speaking to hundreds of students about their plans, dreams, and fears for after college, he wanted to answer a bigger question: how do you live a happy and successful life?

---

1   Dill, David Bruce. "Arlie V. Bock, pioneer in sports medicine. December 30, 1888-August 11, 1984." Medicine and science in sports and exercise 17.3 (1985): 401-404.

So, Bock set out to study the entire lives of hundreds of men.[2] With the help of a benefactor, W.T. Grant, Bock enlisted 268 Harvard students for his study. His goal was to follow them as they went through college, married, retired, and ultimately died. Every few years, Bock's team would track the men's health, happiness, and personal relations.

Early on, two students caught the eye of his research team: Oliver Holmes and Algernon Young.

When Oliver Holmes began his first interview, Bock felt he was destined for success. Holmes grew up in a doting family. He had received music lessons as a child, benefited from private tutoring, and enjoyed parents whom he loved. In an interview with Holmes' mother, she described him as "cooperative and reasonable... he has a delightful sense of humor."

By the time Holmes entered college, he'd become a remarkable young man. He was tall, good-looking, and a member of the debate club. He had close friends and spoke fondly of his family. His jawline was chiseled and his future bright.

Weeks later, the team interviewed another exceptional student: Algernon Young. With a name out of an Oscar Wilde play, he was born for greatness. Like Holmes, Young also grew up in a wealthy family. As his mother described in a later interview, "(Young) was a grown man by the time he was two years old." Of the 268 participants, Young received the highest rating for intellectual gifts and psychological soundness.

---

2   Vaillant, George E. Triumphs of experience. Harvard University Press, 2012.

Your Relationship GPA

Bock flagged students whom he thought would be successful later in life. Early on, he believed that both Young and Holmes would do extremely well.

But, as the pair grew older, their lives quickly diverged. Holmes entered law school, married, and moved close to his family. Professionally, Holmes succeeded marvellously; he became a state judge of Massachusetts, he mentored young lawyers in his free time, and he continued working into his late seventies. His final project was a statewide reform of the legal system.

But, perhaps more impressive than his resume were Holmes' relationships. At eighty-five, Holmes still wrote love poetry for his wife - she painted for him. When required to name intimate friends, he listed six. Even his humor remained intact. When asked about a few prostate problems he'd had, he replied wryly, "My doctor admires its size."

Young faced a different future. At the outset, he had similar, if not greater, potential to Holmes. But, as college went on, his relationships weakened. During his junior year, Young learned his father was battling depression and had been fired from his job. So, to support his family, Young dropped out of Harvard and began working in a factory. The researchers were initially concerned; after all, it was a drastic decision to leave college. But, they were sure he would return after a short break.

Young's father eventually recovered from depression and started working a new job, but Young's personality seemed to have fundamentally changed. At school, he had been popular and outgoing. But, over the course of the next forty years, Young withdrew slowly from his relationships. By forty-nine, his life centered on his pets which kept him "too busy" for others. At fifty-one, his closest friend passed away, never to be replaced. At the age of sixty-six, Algernon Young died. The study rated participants on ten levels of late-life success. He had received a zero.

SUCCESS AFTER COLLEGE

The Grant Study followed the lives of Holmes, Young, and their cohort for over seventy years. During that time, the men graduated, married, and fought in World War II. Some went on to achieve incredible success: of the study participants, four ran for U.S. Senate, and one - John F. Kennedy - became the President of the United States. Others fell in the opposite direction. Many died early, divorced, or grew addicted to alcohol.

Every two years, the director worked with his team to contact the Grant men. Researchers would go to the men's homes and ask them about their lives over the previous years. Questions would range from "How is your health?" to "How often do you have sex?"

As the participants entered their eighties, the third director, George Vaillant, began to look holistically at the lives of these men. As he did, he examined the records from college up until death. In the 1930's, Bock had made predictions about the men's future based upon their wealth, mental acumen, and physical strength; but, as Vaillant found, these guesses were just that, guesses. They were almost no different from random chance.

So, Vaillant continued to search - what factors led to long-life, happiness, and perceived professional success? After ten years, his research culminated in a simple finding; personal relationships mattered more than anything else.

As Valliant put it, "It is social aptitude, not intellectual brilliance or parental social class, that leads to successful aging."[3] Over the course of the study, individuals with strong personal relationships were healthier, happier, and lived longer than their more isolated peers.

Imagine now, if you went back and spoke with that class of sophomores. What would you tell them? Knowing the results of the study, you might advise them to focus more on their friends, their family, and the people around them.

Seventy years later, the similarity between the Grant Study and the lives of millions of college students is too obvious to ignore. And yet, we, as students, never learn about this in school. We're taught how use linear algebra, write in iambic pentameter, and even read Chinese at a first-grade level. But, we're often clueless about the factors that lead to a happy, successful life.

So, we, the authors, began on a quest to understand what the most successful Grant Study men did. In the process, we interviewed dozens of current Harvard students and compared. We focused on personal relationships in college. How did the

---

3   Vaillant, George E. Aging well: Surprising guideposts to a happier life from the landmark study of adult development. Little, Brown, 2008.

best students find friends, make mentors, and expand their personal network?

Our work has culminated into Your Relationship GPA. In it, we have come to a not-too-startling realization: students, by and large, focus on the wrong things in college. Evidence of this abounds at Harvard; students eat alone, give cursory answers to questions like "how are you," and focus on personal success at the expense of deep relationships.

Granted, the Grant Study gives a rather narrow view of "college students." All of the participants were white, male, and attended Harvard. To say that they represent our generation would be both misleading and misinformed. But, if you dive into other research on college students, you'll see that the findings of the Grant Study aren't exceptions to the rule, they are the rule. In studies ranging from first generation students in public universities, to African-American students in primarily black schools, researchers find that relationships drive our success emotionally, physically, and even academically.[4] Regardless of who you are, relationships define your college career.

Unfortunately, the structure of college makes it difficult for students to focus on relationships. We compete on grade point average (GPA) because, frankly, it's the only measurable feedback we receive. Researchers calls this dilemma, "the curse of counting."[5] The theory asserts that we optimize what we can

---

4   Phinney, Jean S, Jessica M Dennis, and Lizette Ivy Chuateco. "The role of motivation, parental support, and peer support in the academic success of ethnic minority first-generation college students." Journal of College Student Development 46.3 (2005): 223-236.

5   Dunn, Elizabeth, and Michael Norton. Happy money: The science of smarter spending. Simon and Schuster, 2013.

count - even if it's not in our long-term interest. People slave away to earn more money, even if doing so doesn't guarantee happiness. The theory focuses on the accumulation of wealth, but the same holds true for GPAs. We manage our grades because we can quantify their movement up and down and compare them with the people around us.

But, what if we're measuring the wrong thing?

The Skills That Matter

As psychologist Daniel Goleman wrote in his landmark book, Emotional Intelligence, your EQ (Emotional Quotient) is a better predictor of success past a certain IQ.[6] Once a college student's intelligence is one standard deviation away from the mean, roughly an IQ of 115-120, adding a few extra IQ points has little effect on long-term success.

Google, for example, recently discovered that two years out of college, grades were no longer predictive of impactful employees. As their head of People Operations put it, "We did a bunch of analysis and found that grades are (slightly) predictive of your first two years, but for the rest of your career don't matter at all."[7]

Your GPA and salary matter, to a point. While they are easy to count, they are not always the best metrics of success.

---

6   Goleman, Daniel. Emotional intelligence. Bantam, 2006.
7   "Do grades matter? Depends if you're asking Google or Goldman - Quartz." 2015. 2 Jun. 2016
<http://qz.com/382570/goldman-sachs-actually-google-gpas-arent-worthless/>

Many students would benefit from focusing more on their interpersonal lives or, as we put it, their Relationship GPA.

In some ways, the idea of focusing on more meaningful metrics isn't unique. We all face a struggle between our external goals and our inner desire to be good, loved, or cared for. David Brooks, author of On the Road to Character, labels these two categories as resume virtues and eulogy virtues. "The résumé virtues are the skills you bring to the job marketplace. The eulogy virtues are the ones that are talked about at your funeral — whether you were kind, brave, honest or faithful. Were you capable of deep love?"[8]

As Brooks makes a distinction between resume virtues and eulogy virtues, we make a distinction between your academic GPA and your Relationship GPA. We fundamentally believe this isn't a tradeoff. As the Grant Study shows, the choice between external and relational success isn't binary. In fact, the students who had the strongest ability to connect with those around them had the most professional success over the course of their life.

How do you become one of those students? As we've found, the difference between Oliver Holmes and Algernon Young can be distilled into five key relationship skills. From vulnerability to taking initiative, mastering these skills will help you succeed in college and beyond.

Research from Duke University shows that habits are most malleable when individuals enter a new environment.[9] Without

8   Brooks, David. The road to character. Random House, 2015.
9   Wood, Wendy, Leona Tam, and Melissa Guerrero Witt. "Changing circumstances, disrupting habits." Journal of personality and social psychology 88.6 (2005): 918.

constraints of the past eighteen years, students need to think critically about themselves. Do I treat people as I should? Would I sacrifice for my friends? And what do I want said at my funeral? College is the time to focus on what matters most.

The mission of Harvard College is "to educate the citizens and citizen-leaders for our society." But, you'll never see a class on how to be a good friend. The same goes for most colleges around the world. If we want to develop stronger relationship skills, we'll have to do it ourselves.

But this leads to an important question: what habits really matter? To understand what skills we'll need to succeed socially in college, we'll have to return to a childhood story. Though few people realize it, Cinderella holds the secret to a higher Relationship GPA.

2

THE CINDERELLA SKILLS

"A dream is a wish your heart makes true."

- Cinderella

We all know the story.

Beautiful, young Cinderella joins a new family when her father remarries. Unfortunately, he soon passes away. Without his protection, her stepmother and stepsisters begin to mistreat her. They force her to wear rags, eat scraps, and clean the house.

Luckily, however, Cinderella can speak with animals. Cinderella's cat frequently assures her "Meow," which Cinderella interprets as, "Cheer up! You have something neither of your stepsisters has and that is beauty." The cat also calls her stepsisters "lumpy," which seems to make things better.

One day, the Prince hosts a ball for all the women in the land. Though Cinderella desperately wants to go, her evil stepmother refuses, instructing her to clean the house while she and her stepsisters are away. As Cinderella cries in her garden, a fairy godmother appears carrying a wand. She smiles broadly; "Don't you worry Cinderella, we'll get you to that ball."

With a wave of her wand, she transforms a pumpkin into a carriage, Cinderella's rags into a gown, and six scurrying mice into a set of horses. The horses neigh, which Cinderella translates as, "My what a beautiful young lady, not lumpy in the least." As the carriage trots away, the fairy godmother gives a final warning: Cinderella must be back by midnight.

Cinderella's entrance to the ball is breathtaking: heads turn, the music slows, and the prince gazes admiringly. Almost immediately, he knows she's the one he's been searching for. Following a protocol that twenty-year-olds in sweaty dorm parties would continue for thousands of years, he asks her if she'd like a drink and a dance. Following a similar protocol, Cinderella tells him "she would love to," but that "she has to leave early." He takes her hand and leads her to the center of the ballroom to dance.

Time flies when you're eligible for marriage but still have a curfew. Hours slip away until suddenly the castle's clock begins to strike, announcing the midnight hour. Cinderella, panicked, runs out of the ballroom to her carriage. In her rush, she leaves a single glass slipper - the only remnant of the night the prince has. He never even learned her name.

The Prince, in an attempt to play it cool, calls for all the kingdom's forces to help him find the owner of the slipper. They go from house to house, asking hundreds of women to try on the lost shoe. When the guards arrive at Cinderella's house, they initially ask only her stepsisters to put on the shoe. After all, Cinderella was wearing rags; she was nothing more than a servant girl. But, the prince's orders had been explicit - "every" lady in the land. So, grudgingly, they ask Cinderella to put on the shoe. It fit perfectly.

Instantly, they guards knew their assumption about Cinderella had been wrong. Without a moment's hesitation, they took Cinderella back to the castle to see the prince. The pair married and, as the story goes, lived happily ever after.

The story of Cinderella should remind us of two things.

One, return lost property after parties. It's your best shot at love.

Two, life is full of diamonds in the rough. More often than not, we're like the guards in the story. We neglect what is truly valuable - Cinderella - and focus on what seems obvious - the well-dressed stepsisters. In college, we often do the same with relationships. We think we know who is important, what matters, and how we should interact with our friends. This is unfortunate because we are often seriously wrong.

CINDERELLA AT COLLEGE

In 1998, linguist David Nunan coined the term "Cinderella Skill" to describe listening. As he put it, "All too often, it has been overlooked by its elder sister: speaking."[1] Nunan is right; students

---

1   Nunan, David. Second Language Teaching & Learning.. Heinle & Heinle Publishers, 7625 Empire Dr., Florence, KY 41042-2978, 1999.

concentrate on an obvious ability, speaking, at the expense of a more meaningful act, listening - but this is not the only common mistake.

Students neglect a series of social skills in college. In Your Relationship GPA, we focus on five vital skills that are often overlooked in practice. Too often we react rather than take initiative (Chapter 3). Speaking is rewarded while listening is forgotten (Chapter 4). Giving is thought to be uncompetitive (Chapter 5). Deadlines are prioritized over rituals (Chapter 6). Perfectionism is flaunted and vulnerability avoided (Chapter 7). We call these topics "The Five Cinderella Skills" of college: traits that matter for successful relationships in school.

Sadly, our K-12 school system has failed us when it comes to teaching social skills. In high school, you can become a "champion orator" in speech and debate. But, you could never win a prize for listening. In your college application, you write a section of "personal accomplishments." But, you would never write about the awards you helped others attain. Our schools value individual achievement. We learn social skills that reflect it.

Luckily, college is a unique opportunity to change how we interact with others. Not only are we in a stage of life where we are always learning, success in college is also tightly linked to your relationships. Your first job, the leadership positions you obtain, and even your grades are profoundly affected by your mentors, friends, and reputation.[2]

---

2 "Korrel Kanoy, Ph.D. - Wiley." 2014. 21 May. 2016 <http://www.wiley.com/legacy/downloads/ Emotional_Intelligence_Learning_What_the_Research_Teaches_Us_About_Its_Importance_to_ Students.pdf>

Social Skills, Not Social Gifts

In 2005, researcher James A. Parker launched the largest study of emotional intelligence and college students ever. In particular, he was interested with the question: how much does your ability to connect with others affect success in college?

He began by recruiting four schools and more than 1400 first-year students.[3] As part of the study, each student took an emotional quotient survey and consented to the researchers reviewing their grades after their first year. The emotional quotient survey measured traits such as interpersonal ability, self-awareness, and adaptability to new situations. Previously, researchers had found that traits like "self-regulation" - better known as the ability to not procrastinate - predicted college GPA. But, they'd never rigorously investigated the effect of your relationships with others.

When Parker came back with the results, his team was shocked. Of all of the traits they'd tested for, interpersonal ability came back as the most predictive of a high GPA. Skills like the ability to empathize, form meaningful social groups, and develop deep relationships all positively related with academic success.

As these results came out, other researchers began to extend upon the findings. During the following ten years, studies would show that interpersonal competence would predict graduation

---

3   Parker, James et al. "Academic achievement and emotional intelligence: Predicting the successful transition from high school to university." Journal of the first-year experience & students in transition 17.1 (2005): 67-78.

rates, friendship quality, and even performance in summer internships.[4]

At first researchers believed that these traits were mostly set from birth. How outgoing, conscientious, or engaging people were seemed like qualities which people had naturally. But, as a few clever studies would show, you can improve these traits with extra work. Sometimes the change is as simple as picking up the right book.

Dr. Jekyll And Mr. Kind

Most students enter medical school with the desire to help people. In a survey of 914 students, almost 90% said their primary reason for entering medicine was "to make a difference."[5] Yet, as time goes on, medical students distance themselves from the people they're trying to help. In particular, when students enter medical rotations in their third and fourth year, the sheer amount of contact with sickness leads students to distance themselves from those in pain. As one researchers suggested, "because students often deal with emotionally challenging and difficult situations, their empathy declines as a protective defense mechanism."[6] Put simply, in the face of suffering, students harden to protect themselves from pain.

---

4   Lievens, Filip et al. "Medical students' personality characteristics and academic performance: A five-factor model perspective." Medical education 36.11 (2002): 1050-1056.

5   "Why Study Medicine? Pre-meds not in it for the money, survey says ..." 2008. 22 May. 2016 <http://www.studentdoctor.net/2008/04/why-study-medicine-pre-meds-not-in-it-for-the-money-survey-says/>

6   THIRIOUX, Berangere, François BIRAULT, and Nematollah JAAFARI. "Empathy is a protective factor of burnout in physicians: new neuro-phenomenological hypotheses regarding empathy and sympathy in care relationship." Frontiers in Psychology 7 (2016): 763.

As doctors distance themselves from their patients, they become less able to help them. For years, the medical field has known that there is a strong connection between doctor-patient relationship and the medical outcome for the patient - as documented in every Grey's Anatomy episode. The more comfortable a patient feels with a doctor, the more likely they are to disclose their entire range of symptoms. The more a doctor can empathize with patients, the more deeply they're able to understand the underlying sickness.[7] Though medical school teaches the skills necessary to become a doctor, it inadvertently degrades another: the ability to connect with others.

In the early 2000's, UC Irvine professor Johanna Shapiro wanted to understand whether she could change empathy levels in medical students. So, she recruited twenty first year medical students for a literature course especially designed to increase empathy. The curriculum consisted of eight small-group reading and discussion sections for one hour. The class taught poetry, skits, and short-stories that addressed topics common to doctors: doctor-patient relationship, physical examinations, listening to pain, sexuality, etc. During the course, the researchers placed special emphasis on identifying with the patient's point of view.

The researchers measured empathy at the beginning and end of the semester. As they found, even their small intervention had a significant effect on the students. Unlike most medical students, whose empathy decreases with time, students in

---

7   Hojat, Mohammadreza et al. "Empathy in medical students as related to academic performance, clinical competence and gender." Medical education 36.6 (2002): 522-527.

the literature class reported a deeper ability to relate to their patients.[8]

However, it's not just empathy that we can change. Countless studies have shown that we can improve skills like managing stress, listening to others, and building strong relationships.[9] As Stanford psychologist Carol Dweck put it, "there's a lot of intelligence out there being wasted by underestimating students' potential to develop."[10] The same is true of your social intelligence. The more you practice, the better you get.

For the remainder of this book, we'll focus on "The Five Cinderella Skills" - skills that are essential to master as a college student. Along the way, you'll learn why we like great listeners more than we like great speakers, how people who help others succeed faster, and why we view those who are vulnerable as stronger than those who never express self-doubt.

As a disclaimer, if attempting any of the Cinderella Skills ever feels forced, sit the opportunity out - there will be plenty more. The more you practice, the more natural applying these skills will become. Make sure you feel comfortable every time.

You won't improve all at once. But, you don't need to. After Prince Charming "found" - please read "stole" - the glass slipper, he searched every house in the kingdom to find Cinderella. He

---

8   Shapiro, J. "Teaching empathy to first year medical students: evaluation of ... - NCBI." 2004. <http://www.ncbi.nlm.nih.gov/pubmed/15203476>
9   Schutte, Nicola, and John Malouff. "Incorporating emotional skills content in a college transition course enhances student retention." Journal of the First-Year Experience & Students in Transition 14.1 (2002): 7-21.
10   Dweck, Carol. Mindset: The new psychology of success. Random House, 2006.

experimented, he failed, and then he tried again. Given enough discipline and determination, he found what he was looking for. We hope that you'll do the same.

TAKE INITIATIVE

LISTEN WELL

BE VULNERABLE

MAKE RITUALS

GIVE OFTEN

3

TAKE INITIATIVE

"Showing up is 80 percent of life."

- Woody Allen

Nina Hooper paced frantically in her Harvard dorm room.[1]

"How could I meet Richard Branson?" She thought aloud. She didn't live in London. She didn't have millions to donate. And Nancy, Richard's secretary, had proved to be a more impenetrable wall than she had hoped.

Not to be defeated, Nina turned to her faithful friend: Google.

"Where is Richard Branson?" she typed. Scrolling through results, she found a recent post on his twitter. He was spending the next few days in his Caribbean home, Necker Island. Suddenly, Nina knew what she needed to do.

---

1   Hooper, N (2016, January 15) Personal Interview

She opened another tab and searched for flights to the British Virgin Islands. It looked like she'd miss physics class that week.

Nina Hooper isn't your standard college student. She's an Australian astrophysicist with an unmatched hunger for challenge. Her passion for space led her to be the first student to speak at TedXHarvardCollege, where she presented her research on the economic feasibility of asteroid mining. Like many children, Nina wanted to be an astronaut. But rather than letting her dreams erode with thoughts of job safety and big paychecks, she focused on her love of physics and was admitted to Harvard. During her sophomore year, she almost made it to space. Almost. How? Nina was brave in the face of rejection.

WHY HEARING "NO" HURTS SO BAD

Rejection, very literally, hurts. In a 2003 FMRI study, researchers from UCLA found that social rejection elicits the same neurological reaction as physical pain.[2] In their study, they asked participants to play a virtual game of catch. The game consisted of three players passing a digital ball between them. The researchers strapped the participant to an FMRI machine and assigned them player one. Researchers then told the subject that players two and three were controlled by two other participants in another room. Secretly though, they were programmed computers.

---

2   Eisenberger, Naomi I, Matthew D Lieberman, and Kipling D Williams. "Does rejection hurt? An fMRI study of social exclusion." Science 302.5643 (2003): 290-292.

At first, each player received the ball evenly. The human participant passed to player two, two passed to three, and three returned the ball to the participant. Then after seven throws, the participant stopped receiving the ball. Player two and player three passed the ball back and forth for the next forty-five turns. The computers excluded the participant. If you could read player two and three's lifeless digital expressions, you would just know they were having more fun.

The participant's FMRI told a story of pain. Their anterior cingulate cortex - the part of the brain that registers physical discomfort - had higher levels of activity when excluded from playing. As the researchers found, social rejection activated the same neurological pathways as being physically hit.

Our instinctual fear of social rejection makes breaking social norms challenging. Imagine, for illustration, that you're in a room with seven other people. Imposing scientists in white lab coats stand in the front of the room next to a projector. The screen shows four lines: one line labeled "reference" on a card by itself, and three lines labeled a, b, and c to its right. The researchers ask you to pick one of the three lines that is closest in length to the reference.

It's obvious, you think to yourself; it's clearly line c.

The researchers ask each person one-by-one to state the matching line. They start with the person on the opposite end of you. "Line a!" the first participant confidently exclaims.

"How weird," you think. You're sure it's line c.

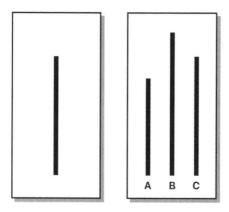

The next participant is up. "Line a!" she says.

By this time you're looking back at the image carefully. You're sure c is the right length.

The researchers ask each of the other seven participants. They all say line a. When it's your turn to answer, you stare confused at the projection. Seven people can't all be wrong... can they?

In 1951, psychologist Solomon Asch performed a similar study on college students. He placed seven confederates, or fake participants, in the room with the instruction to choose the wrong line every time. He then measured the number of times that the actual subjects changed under social pressure. Alone students almost never picked the wrong line. When placed with social pressures, however, participants conformed nearly one out of every three trials. More than seventy-five percent of participants conformed at least once during the experiment.

When asked why they chose the wrong line, people often gave a blunt answer: they didn't want to disagree publicly with the entire group.[3]

Our fear of rejection has an evolutionary basis.[4] Before agriculture, most individuals lived in a tribe of fewer than a hundred people. In these small communities, there were lifelong repercussions to embarrassing first impressions. Thousands of years of evolution hardwired nervous butterflies into our stomach when approaching someone new.

Unfortunately, this fear is misplaced in a modern college. You might meet more than a hundred people at a single event. If you mess up with one person, you'll both move on. Sending an email to a professor, asking a classmate on a date, or inviting friends to hang out might feel scary - but to control your social life, you'll have to master that fear. You'll need to make the first step.

Here's the key: the world rarely comes to you. You might go an entire semester before someone in class introduces themselves. You might eat lunch alone every day wishing someone would approach you to talk. And unless you know your subject better than your professor, it is unlikely they will single you out for mentorship. Waiting for others is conforming. It's more comfortable. It's saying that the lines are the same length.

---

3   Asch, Solomon E. "Effects of group pressure upon the modification and distortion of judgments." Groups, leadership, and men. S (1951): 222-236.

4   Croston, Glenn. The real story of risk: adventures in a hazardous world. Prometheus Books, 2012.

Long-term, however, it's a dangerous choice. If you don't decide your social life, someone else will for you.

W. W. N. D. (What. Would. Nina. Do.)

During her sophomore year of college, Nina hatched a plan to win a trip to space. At the time, the only way a civilian could enter space was through a few private companies; British billionaire Richard Branson offered one avenue in the form of Virgin Galactic.

Branson founded the company in 2004 with the intention of offering commercial space flights for adventurous passengers. Unfortunately, to reserve a future spot, Virgin Galactic required a down payment of two hundred and fifty thousand dollars. Nina didn't have that money, but she did have a magnificent amount of initiative.

In 2014, Virgin Galactic partnered with Land Rover "to send the most adventurous people it [could] find into space."[5] The marketing contest required applicants to submit images or a thirty-second video demonstrating the spirit of adventure. The winning candidate would earn a trip to space along with three friends. Nina was an adventurer; she merely had to prove her spirit to win a trip to space.

Nina realized that to her, adventure meant finding things that make you excited. What excited her most was Richard Branson himself. Unfortunately, the eccentric entrepreneur was

5   "Land Rover, Virgin Galactic Launch Competition to Send ... - Space.com." 2014. 2 Jun. 2016 <http://www.space.com/27127-land-rover-virgin-galactic-space-competition.html>

not easy to reach. He travelled around the world managing the Virgin Group, a multinational conglomerate worth billions of dollars. Virgin's impenetrable wall of assistants and procedures stood between Nina and Richard Branson.

It was, however, possible for wealthy individuals to meet Richard Branson. In 1978, the British Virgin island Necker was for sale at the bargain price of six million dollars. Imagining the island as a means of wooing rock stars for his record label - and perhaps personal dates - young Richard Branson visited the island and fell in love. He lowballed the six million dollar asking price, offering to buy the island for one hundred and fifty thousand dollars.[6] Though the offer was initially rejected with laughter, the later broke owner, Lord Cobham, eventually sold the island to Branson for one hundred and eighty thousand dollars.

The island came with an unusual government stipulation. Its new owner had five years to develop a resort or else the land would return to the hands of the state. With great speed and expense, the extravagant Necker Island resort was born. For a modest cost of more than two thousand dollars a night, guests could experience bamboo furniture from Bali, 360-degree views of the island from their bedrooms, and service from more than one hundred staff members. Richard Branson loved the resort so much, he'd frequent it on holidays and even chat with the guests that happened to stay there.

---

6   "Richard Branson: How I Bought Necker Island - Virgin." 2015. 2 Jun. 2016 <https://www.virgin.com/richard-branson/how-i-bought-necker-island>

Your Relationship GPA

Necker Island was Nina's one chance to meet Richard Branson in person. Unfortunately, her limited college budget could not afford a night stay on the island. She needed to be creative. She needed to do something illegal enough to get his attention, but not so criminal that she would be arrested. She needed to sneak on the island.

Nina's first idea was an assault by air. She reached out to all nearby skydiving companies, as we assume anyone in her position would. Over the phone, she explained the competition and why they needed to let her skydive onto Necker Island. Unfortunately, no company was willing to help her land on private property, particularly that of a respected and highly guarded resort.

Nina's second idea was a remote assault by air. From the relative safety of an offshore boat, she planned to pilot a drone to the island and have it deliver a small gift for Richard Branson. To do so, however, she would need a boat.

Nina called every boat company within range of Necker Island. Again, she faced a similar problem - what she was asking for was too risky for any business to consent. They did, however, point her in the direction of one man who might be able to help.

Gumption, a Rastafarian, was a local to the Virgin Islands. Using a small loan from Richard Branson he had bought a glass bottom boat that he proudly used to give tours around Necker Island. No one was in a better position to assist Nina, but getting in touch with Gumption proved tricky - he lacked a website.

Luckily, like any good glass-bottom-boat-entrepreneur, he had an active Twitter account.

Nina took a digital first step by emailing the small tour company and tweeting at the company's Twitter account. Gumption and his assistant bounced Nina back and forth, ignoring her pleas for a short conversation. Still, she was not discouraged. Using the camera on her laptop, Nina made a short video in which she introduced herself, explained the competition, and asked for help.

What Was Your Name Again?

Though few of us will attempt to skydive onto private property, we all have opportunities to take initiative. One key way to take initiative is to reach out to new people. Though scary, it will become one of the most important skills you pick up in college.

Unfortunately, reaching out to new people is something even professionals do poorly. A study at Columbia University found that at networking mixers, attendees almost exclusively spoke with people they already knew or who they had a mutual connection with.[7] This behavior contradicts their stated reason for attending: to meet new people. Similarly, you likely attend college to make new connections. How can you break the barrier to meet someone new?

---

7   Casciaro, Tiziana, Francesca Gino, and Maryam Kouchaki. "The Contaminating Effects of Building Instrumental Ties How Networking Can Make Us Feel Dirty." *Administrative Science Quarterly* (2014): 0001839214554990.

Part of the answer lies in becoming better at names. According to a survey by the British gaming company Ladbrokes, people rated forgetting someone's name during an introduction as their number one most embarrassing moment.[8] This is bad news because in college you'll forget hundreds, if not thousands, of names over the course of four years.

Luckily, few people are naturally bad at remembering names. As researchers from Kansas State discovered, the belief that "I am bad at learning names" is mostly a myth.[9] Instead, the difference lies in our motivation levels. As their experiments showed, people who remembered names best reported a higher motivation to want to learn other names, not more mental power. Teachers and politicians, for example, learned names because they believed it crucial to their success. As the researchers argued, "It's not necessarily your brain's ability that determines how well you can remember names, but rather your level of interest." Learning names is a matter of effort, not innate talent.

One strategy to remember others' names is to repeat them in conversation. Certain memorization apps capitalize on this by using timed repetition to improve recall. Underlying the technology is an insight into memory: we learn best what we repeat often. Take, for example, this imaginary conversation.

---

8   Rollag, Keith. What to Do when You're New: How to be Comfortable, Confident, and Successful in New Situations. AMACOM Div American Mgmt Assn, 2015.

9   "News Releases - Kansas State University." 2014. 3 Jun. 2016 <https://www.k-state.edu/media/newsreleases/jun12/memory62012.html>

"Hey, what did you say your name was again? I see you in biology all the time!"

"My name's Mark Zuckerberg."

"Oh, awesome. So, Mark, did you get the notes last lecture?"

And so on.

Echoing someone's name places it in short-term memory which helps solidify the memory long-term.[10] Experts give a range of the number of times you should say someone's name: somewhere from three to seven. Regardless of the specifics, repeat your partner's name while talking. If you do forget, ask again with a self-deprecating laugh until you remember. Make it an inside joke that you can't remember their name. As you do, you'll change no-name strangers into acquaintances you begin to know.

In college, there are no shortage of these no-name strangers for you to practice with. If you don't know the person sitting next to you in lecture, start there. "Morning, how's it going? Did you do the reading last night?" As soon as they have responded and engaged you in a conversation, say the magic words: "I'm sorry, what did you say your name was again?"

This phrasing "What was your name again?" is particularly useful. Maybe they already told you their name, though likely they haven't. Either way, this question assumes you've forgotten. In doing so, it humbly admits that you don't always remember names, but that you want to try.

---

10   Foer, Joshua. Moonwalking with Einstein: The art and science of remembering everything. Penguin, 2011.

Not everyone feels comfortable starting conversations with new people. Luckily, there are ways that we can overcome this anxiety. One strategy is to make people come to you, as demonstrated by a very brave freshman.

Why The Ukulele?

When students describe Ana Olano, they use phrases like "Ana is the most outgoing person I know," "It's hard not to be friends with Ana," and "How do you spell her name?" People know her for her passion for science, her love of others, and a monthly show she MCs - Coffeehouse. But, if you spoke with Ana, she'd say she wasn't always successful socially.

Early in high school, Ana wasn't envied for her relationships. "Around middle school, I really held my shell close to me,"[11] she says. Social anxiety would cause her to freeze up when speaking to classmates, and she struggled to make good first impressions. Ana loved science, but that love failed to reserve her a spot among the popular girls.

"I'd look around and see people interacting so easily, and I'd wonder why I couldn't fit into that scene." She tried searching online for tips on how to socialize, but she quickly realized that "people are not a mathematical formula." Paradoxically, it seemed the only way to get better at approaching people would be to do just that - approach people.

---

11   Olano, A. (2016, January 14th). Personal Interview

Ana could have started small: perhaps by talking to one new person a week. However, Ana is not the sort of woman to make small changes to her life. Instead, she swung for the fences and brought a ukulele to school.

Ana's natural musical talent and Google's plethora of tutorials helped her quickly learn how to play basic chords on the instrument. It was too large to fit in her book bag, so she was forced to carry it by hand everywhere she went. Students would glance at her, look away, and then look back. "Why the ukulele?" they would ask. Suddenly, conversations with strangers began opening themselves. She was talking to new people every day, and they couldn't help but remember her because their second question was always the same: "Can you play a song?"

Ana would force herself to play whenever someone asked. Luckily, most mortals cannot help but smile when they hear Israel Kamakawiwoʻole's Somewhere Over The Rainbow. Many people know the lyrics, and an even larger percentage know how to hum. As Ana played, she'd find herself surrounded by strangers singing along. After they finished, they'd introduce themselves to Ana and thank her for the song. For Ana, publicly playing music changed her fear around approaching others. She noticed that not only was she improving socially, but she was also bringing joy to all the people around her. That shift in perspective made public performances all the easier. After playing ukulele to impromptu groups of twenty strangers, asking for someone's name became trivial.

Think creatively about how to bring others to you. We're not suggesting buy a ukulele, however, the example of Ana shows that you can help others make the first step.

Gumption Pulls Through

Nina's creative video message was enough to make Gumption, the tour boat captain, come to her. He was quick to respond, saying: "lol girl you have my attention. I'm blown away! I think I'm going to make it happens!" Nina was thrilled - she had an in. She used her savings to purchase a plane ticket to Miami, and then to the Virgin Islands. Donning a cheap black suit, she packed her bag and started filming.

After she had landed in the Virgin Islands, she found her way onto a small yacht that brought her to Gumption. He in turn brought her to Necker Island and gave her a private tour where she played with tortoises, lemurs, and flamingos. All the while, she filmed herself with a tripod.

The one thing she didn't find on the island was Richard Branson. The man had left only hours before she arrived. Resilient as ever, Nina finished filming and returned home. The resulting thirty-second video tells it all.[12] Its portrayal of Nina as a cheesy spy breaking onto Richard Branson's private island captured the exact spirit of adventure that the competition was seeking.

---

12 "necker adventure extended nina | #lostintheworld - YouTube." 2014. 7 Jun. 2016 <https://www.youtube.com/watch?v=ITT03EEEPTs>

Word of her escapade made its way to Branson and he tweeted at her "@ninalhooper just saw your video, great work & sorry we missed you on Necker. Best of luck with your start-up too!"[13] She was over the moon to have received a direct compliment from her personal hero. The competition also enjoyed her video, deeming her the deserving victor. The company placed Nina among movie stars and CEOs on the waitlist for space travel.

Then, tragedy struck. In October 2014, a Virgin Galactic rocket broke apart in a test flight. The pilot was severely injured, and the co-pilot did not survive.[14] The competition rules were forced to be revised, and Nina instead enjoyed a week with three friends living in a castle in England. While a castle is no space flight for an astrophysicist, it still proved to be a spectacular reward for Nina's effort. More valuable though, was the adventure she had and the people she met along the way. While ukuleles and Caribbean adventures are spectacular ways to meet people, often the simplest of college rituals can be the best starting points.

We Should Grab A Meal Sometime

There is an old Irish proverb, "Laughter is brightest in the place where the food is." Eating with other people is one of the best ways to bond with others. In fact, there are entire books

---

13   "Richard Branson on Twitter: "@ninalhooper just saw your video, great ..."" 2014. 3 Jun. 2016 <https://twitter.com/richardbranson/status/524860560492331008>

14   "Virgin Galactic's SpaceShipTwo Crashes in Test Flight, 1 ... - Space.com." 2014. 3 Jun. 2016 <http://www.space.com/27618-virgin-galactic-spaceshiptwo-crash-kills-pilot.html>

written on the subject - check out Keith Ferrazzi's Never Eat Alone for a great primer. Once you know the name of the people you bump into on a daily basis, why not eat with them? In the next few paragraphs, we'll detail one way to use meals to make the first step.

First, simply ask someone out to breakfast, lunch, or dinner. "We should grab a meal sometime; I'd love to hear your thoughts on skydiving into the property of eccentric billionaires." They'll probably agree; you should grab a meal sometime! At this point, take the next step. Put a date on the books. "How about Tuesday at noon at Al's sandwich shop?" Day, time, place. Once they agree, pull out your calendar and add the event. Grab their phone number too if you don't already have it.

Next, make sure you set a reminder. An hour before the meal, send them a message to double check that they are still free to come. If they cancel, reschedule. Master asking people to meals, and you'll set yourself up for numerous meaningful connections.

One-on-one conversations are great, but they're not the only way to take initiative. Some of college's best memories come from hanging out with a group of friends. Maybe you go to a late night movie, order pizza for a facade of a study group, or embark on a failed quest to find a party. These are the sorts of events that create lasting memories. But, they don't create themselves. You'll need to learn how to start a group event yourself.

Groups constantly suffer from the chicken-before-the-egg problem. How do get the first few people to come? Social psychology shows that it is hardest for the first person to commit. Imagine being invited to a party. When you ask who else is coming, they reply, "Only you so far." You probably don't want to go.

So, how do you convince a group of people to go on an adventure? You need an exciting activity, a compelling reason, and most importantly: a group-starting tactic. To improve your ability to initiate group events, we'll show you the "Shock and Aww" strategy. Its origins lie a long time ago, in a galaxy far, far away....

STAR WARS & "THE SHOCK AND AWW" STRATEGY

For those who haven't seen Star Wars, here's a brief primer to bring you up to speed.

Jedi are rogue vigilantes who use laser swords to cut people in half. They also wear long bathrobes.

The Republic is a benevolent inter-planetary government. Imagine Athens, but with more tentacles.

Chancellor Palpatine is the leader of the republic. He is secretly a Sith Lord - Darth Sidious. That means he also cuts people in half. His preferred bathrobe is a slimming black.

At the end of the third movie, Chancellor Palpatine executes Order 66. At the time, he controls a clone army for the Republic. The order triggers an attack on Jedi knights and their Jedi temple.

George Lucas called the attack, "Operation Knightfall." He did not win the Oscar for best screenwriting.

Thousands of clones descend upon the temple. They kill everyone inside - from rogue vigilantes to child-versions of rogue vigilantes. With total disregard for fabulous architecture, the clones set fire to the Jedi Temple.

After the initial attack, Order 66 commands the clone army to individually pick off the remaining Jedi. Identical versions of Temuera Morrison move throughout the galaxy to find stragglers. The ratio of dark to light bathrobes shifts perceptibly to the dark. The only survivors are Obi-Wan Kenobi - a white, old man - and Yoda - a green, dyslexic humanoid.

Operation Knightfall can teach us two things: one, the dangers of not installing effective security systems and two, the steps of the "Shock and Aww…" strategy for creating groups events.

SHOCK

Order 66 began with a massive attack. Chancellor Palpatine wanted to destroy as many Jedi at once. The assault on the temple eliminated the majority of his targets.

Similarly, the first step to planning a social event is to notify a relatively large group. For concreteness, let's say you want to throw a cookie-making party for friends. You'd like ten people to come together for the love of snickerdoodle. You've never thrown an event before, but you've seen enough Star Wars to know how it's done.

Begin by inviting a large group of people all at once. If you have a friend group chat, reach out to the group saying, "Hey guys, make cookies with me Friday night! I'll be in the dorm kitchen." If you don't have a pre-made group, create one yourself. Send a message to a collection of people that you like, and who vaguely know each other. This first step accomplishes two things. By creating a group, you show that this event is for multiple people. Second, you allow the other people to see who else might be attending.

Aww...

The second part of Order 66 was the clone attack on straggling Jedi. Instead of laying siege to the entire galaxy, they individually targeted light-bathrobed persons on each planet.

Similarly, the next step of "Shock and Aww..." is to reach out personally. We call this the "Aww..." portion because it demonstrates that you care about the individual attending, thus eliciting an "Aww..." noise. In the case of the snickerdoodle party, individually message every person in the group chat. For example, say "Hey John, I really liked talking with you yesterday about Darth Sidious - man he's a terrible galactic emperor! LOL. Anyways, I'd love to see you at the cookie party tomorrow. Can you make it?"

The purpose of individually reaching out is that it shifts the level of responsibility. If you ask a large group, people feel less compelled to join. In psychology, this is called the bystander effect. It occurs when responsibility feels diluted across a group. No one member feels compelled to step up for an activity.[15]

When you personally reach out, responsibility shifts from the group to the individual. The question changes from "Would this 'activity' be fun?" to "Do I want to spend time with my friend?" People feel a deeper commitment to individuals than to events. Every time you reach out, you make that person significantly more likely to attend.

Experiment with the strategy. Some people prefer "Aww... and Shock." They reach out individually. Then when they have a few people confirmed, they tell a larger group. In our experience, both work well. What's most important is the combination of both the group (Shock) and the individual (Aww) invitation.

Regrettably, not all social interactions are positive. College will throw you into an unpredictable environment with new people. Given enough time, you'll face moments where you annoy your friends and your friends bother you. To avoid conflicts, you'll once again need to refer to the Cinderella Skills and take the first step.

---

15 "Bystander Effect | Psychology Today." 2015. 3 Jun. 2016 <https://www.psychologytoday.com/basics/bystander-effect>

YOU AND YOUR NORDIC ROOM

When you face conflict, be the first to act. Often disputes boil beneath the surface of college relationship. You might be annoyed with a messy roommate. She might be angry at your late bedtime. If neither of you address the problem, you'll endanger your relationship.

The first step often involves bringing light to an unspoken irritation. Take the case of the messy roommate.

For the most part, you love your dorm room companion. She's fun, adventurous, and shares your strange love of Icelandic music. She's perfect. On your first night together, you make a plan for the room. You'll take the left half and decorate it with pictures of your family, friends, and Jón Þór Birgisson. She'll take the right half and decorate it with posters of her hometown, favorite sports team, and Ragnar Þórhallsson. As the posters go up, you gaze fondly around your Nordic room.

A few weeks into the semester and you notice the right side of the room beginning to transform. Drawers that used to close remain open. Posters peel from an untouched wall. You thought the top of her desk was wooden, but under dust, papers, and empty wrappers you really can't tell. You're a little concerned. You love cleanliness almost as much as you love the vocal riffs of Georg Hólm, but you don't want to cause a fight.

You decide to brush it off. Besides, the first few weeks of college are busy. Perhaps she'll change when the semester calms down.

Two months later and the bedroom is now a war zone. Socks hang from the fire alarm. Pizza boxes plug the front door. You once saw a tentacle slither from a clothing pile. As you walk to your bed, you slip on a mound of jam. That's when you know. You and your roommate need to talk.

Raising a grievance is difficult, but there are ways to make the act painless. First, try to address your concern as early as possible. Likely, your disapproval is less obvious than you think. The more explicit you are, the easier you make it for others to change. In the case of your roommate, she might not know how much you care about cleanliness. By being explicit, you give her the opportunity to change her behavior.

Give feedback at the appropriate time. You should initiate most conversations like this in private, at a time when outside deadlines and stressors are low.[16] This means after a final exam, not the night before. Spend the time leading up to the conversation building affiliation by talking about common backgrounds, challenges, and Nordic vocalists.

Create a positive environment through honest statements of appreciation - if you do in fact have a close relationship, there should be countless things to be thankful for. In longitudinal studies of married couples, pairs that maintain a ratio of at least five positive comments to every one negative comment are most likely to remain married.[17] You're not married to your roommate,

16   Fisher, Roger, William L Ury, and Bruce Patton. Getting to yes: Negotiating agreement without giving in. Penguin, 2011.
17   Gottman, John M et al. "Predicting marital happiness and stability from newlywed interactions." Journal of Marriage and the Family (1998): 5-22.

but judging by the amount you share toiletries, bicker over who made what mess, and failure to ever sleep together, you might as well be.

Once you've created a positive environment, bring light to the dispute. Here only nuanced communication will help you and your roommate come to a resolution - but you are communicating because you took the first step, and that is what matters. Taking initiative is vital not only for starting relationships, but ensuring that they last.

"No" Means "Try Someone Else"

In the case of Nina Hooper, taking the first step changed her life. She spoke with dozens of skydiving companies, boating agencies, and tour companies. Each time that she reached out, she grew closer to her goal.

Nina instinctively knew that speaking to the companies would not be enough. Most of the people she messaged would reject her request. She was right. They did. Of the 20+ people that she cold-called, only Gumption was willing to help her get to the island. So, instead of stopping at "no," Nina asked for two things. First, why wouldn't they help her and two, who would they suggest talking to next?

With each rejection, she sought first to understand. Why wouldn't they let her skydive? Well, because it was private property. Why wouldn't the tour guide take her? Because he didn't have the license. Who did have the license?

Little by little, the conversations brought her to Gumption. One skydiving company suggested a local boating company. A boating firm suggested a tour guide. Finally, a tour guide suggested that Nina reach out to Gumption. Slowly, a series of connections brought Nina to her destination.

Her key was listening. This forgotten skill helped her connect unknown dots. With each failed conversation, she didn't grow farther from her goal. She grew closer. As we'll see, the power of listening wasn't unique to Nina's situation. It's a skill that profoundly influences our entire life - especially in college.

TAKE INITIATIVE

LISTEN WELL

BE VULNERABLE

MAKE RITUALS

GIVE OFTEN

Your Relationship GPA

4
LISTEN WELL

"Most people do not listen with the intent to understand, they listen with the intent to reply."

- Stephen Covey

The doorbell rang.[1]

Instantly, Nate and Zoey stopped talking. Their legs, draped casually over chairs, tensed. Their eyes locked, and they each took a breath.

Even with experience, every night's first stranger always invited butterflies.

Zoey stood up first. As she walked to the front of the room, she mentally primed herself for the conversation ahead. Arriving at the door, she placed her hand slowly on the knob. She was ready to counsel.

Zoey opened the door. "Welcome to Room 13."

---

1   Room 13 is a confidential, anonymous resource at Harvard College. The story, all names, characters, and incidents portrayed in this chapter are fictitious. No identification with actual persons, events, or relationships is intended or should be inferred.

The student, standing in the doorway, didn't reply at first. Instead, her bloodshot eyes roamed through the room. They passed over a jar of cookies, a wall of sex ed pamphlets, and Nate, still sitting in his chair. Cautiously, the student stepped in.

"Would you like to talk?" Nate asked, now standing.

The student nodded. Her hands were plunged deep into her jean pockets. Nate motioned for her to follow Zoey into another room.

This new room was identical to the first, except for a large, purple couch in the center. Facing the couch were two equally purple chairs in which Nate and Zoey took seats. The student moved to sit on the couch.

Before the familiar sound of silence could fill the room, Nate spoke.

"So, how are you feeling?"

THE ROOM 13 MODEL

In the basement of Thayer Hall at Harvard, there's a room called "Room 13." Every night from 7:00 PM to 7:00 AM, a pair of anonymous Harvard undergrads sit, waiting to talk to anyone who knocks on their door. The group is part peer counseling group and part urban legend. Students know the staff as the best listeners on campus.

In 1970, Margaret Mckenna, a recent graduate of Harvard's sister school Radcliffe College, founded Room 13 as a drug response line. In the years following its creation, the group transformed into a generalized counseling group. Of the 30+ undergraduate staffers, two would sit in Room 13 every night and wait for Harvard students to drop-in with problems, questions, or with the simple urge to talk. Topics range from freshman stresses to suicidal thoughts.[2]

In many ways, Harvard students try to project a perfect version of themselves. Though this helps them appear confident, it serves as a double-edged sword. Students rarely speak openly about their struggles. Instead, they wall themselves off behind visages of success, strength, or simply busyness ("I wish I could talk, but I have…"). It takes true courage for students to go to a place like Room 13 and bare their problems for strangers to hear.

Interestingly, Room 13 has become one of the most successful organizations at Harvard College. In a school where clubs typically survive three to five years, Room 13 has existed in much the same form for nearly fifty. As Mckenna put it, "The structure then was pretty much identical to the way it is now. There is a guy and a girl that sit in the room from 7:00 PM to 7:00 AM. From the very beginning, we had a weekly meeting where we discussed counseling. Even the phone number is the same."[3]

Each year, 100+ students apply to become counselors, of which around fifteen are selected for training. The proven value

2   "Room 13: A Little Help From Their Friends | News | The Harvard Crimson." 2009. 3 Jun. 2016 <http://www.thecrimson.com/article/1974/9/27/Room 13-a-little-help-from/>
3   Mckenna, M. (June 11, 2016) Personal Interview

of Room 13 has even inspired similar efforts: since 1970, Harvard students have formed five counseling groups that imitate Room 13's model, ranging in topic from sexual assault to eating disorders.

What has made Room 13 such a positive presence at Harvard?

They have a unique approach to listening.

Before school begins, Room 13 trains its counselors to become "nondirective, nonjudgmental" listeners. In practice, this means that counselors rarely offer their opinions, stories, or suggestions. Instead, they ask questions, make clarifying statements, or simply give sounds of affirmation. They are taught to almost never reference themselves in conversation. Their goal is one minded: to understand and empathize with whomever they listen to.

The Original Cinderella Skill

Listening is perhaps the single most overlooked skill in school. David Nunan called "listening" the original Cinderella skill because we emphasize speaking at its expense. This is a shame, because when it comes to developing relationships, listening is a much more important factor.

According to Princeton psychology professor Diana Tamir, talking about yourself offers a short-term chemical reward.[4] The

---

4   Tamir, Diana I, and Jason P Mitchell. "Disclosing information about the self is intrinsically rewarding." Proceedings of the National Academy of Sciences 109.21 (2012): 8038-8043.

neural activity associated with self-disclosure mimics that of eating and sex. Simply put, people love talking about their life. When we listen well, we make others feel great.

Encouraging people to speak about themselves isn't difficult. One of the experiments developed by Professor Tamir offered participants varying amounts of money to answer questions of their choice. They could choose to answer fact-based questions and maximize their earnings, or answer questions about themselves for a lower reward. On average, people were willing to give up seventeen percent of potential earnings to answer self-centered questions. People are literally willing to lose money to keep the focus on themselves.

Not only do people love personal attention, most are also notoriously bad at listening to others. The study noted that an average person spends roughly forty percent of conversations talking about themselves. Ironically, few people are aware of how that same breakdown applies to them. As an experiment, ask a friend about their average role in a conversation. More likely than not, they'll say that they listen a higher percentage of the time than they speak.

Now, ask yourself the same question: how much of a conversation do you spend genuinely interested in the other side? Perhaps you fear that if you rarely talk about yourself, your conversational buddy won't feel a sense of connection to you. Ironically, the exact opposite is true. When people talk about themselves in a conversation, they generally leave feeling like they know and trust the other side more.

Being a good listener means doing more than asking a lot of questions. Doing that can lead to awkward, interview-like conversations. Instead, you need to stay active, yet non-directive. Room 13 counselors constantly practice this careful balance.

I Can't Imagine

"So, how are you feeling?"

Nate's question hung in the air until the nervous student spoke.

"I need your advice."

Slowly at first, she explained that her ex-boyfriend had been contacting her frequently and that she was confused about the situation. She still had feelings for him, but she'd wanted to make a clean break after they separated. Immediately Nate's instinct was to relate back to his own experiences - he'd just broken up with his girlfriend too. He had to stop himself from interjecting. Thinking back to training, he remembered the Room 13 adage "The conversation isn't about you." Nate might have had a similar experience, but he didn't know exactly how the student was feeling. He instead asked a question.

"You mentioned that you feel conflicted, could you tell us what that feels like?"

The nervous drop-in returned to her story. She did feel conflicted. On one hand, she had promised her friends that she wouldn't talk to her ex. She had experienced painful off-and-on relationships before and was determined not to go back.

On the other hand, she still had feelings for him. They'd broken up partly because she'd left last semester to study abroad. She'd always really liked him, and six months hadn't changed that.

Finally, she'd gone on a few dates with a new guy recently. Was it immoral to pursue both of them at once? They hadn't talked about being exclusive, and yet that seemed to weigh on her mind.

As she finished the story, she turned to the pair. "What should I do?"

That was a lot all at once; each sentence the student had spoken was packed with immense nuance. At this point, some people might offer advice that worked for them in the past, or they might unconsciously talk about a similarly challenging experience. In Room 13, however, counselors rarely believe they fully understand a problem. Instead of giving advice, they try to understand the issue at a deeper level.

Zoey artfully replied, "I can't imagine what you're feeling right now." Instead of giving suggestions, she tried to reframe the question for the drop-in to answer.

"It sounds like part of you feels very logical. What would your logical self do in this situation?"

The drop-in replied, "She'd probably not interact with her ex."

"Okay." Zoey answered, "It also sounds like part of you still has feelings of affection - is that right? What would your romantic self do?"

Again, the drop-in made a prediction. Her romantic self would ask him to go with her on a long walk. After Zoey stepped through the two most prominent selves, she asked about several others: scared self, angry self, and lonely self. Slowly, the drop-in began to answer her own question.

BECOMING A BETTER LISTENER

Room 13 counselors visualize conversations like a series of doors.[5] The counselor doesn't force the drop-in to speak about anything. Instead, counselors "knock on doors," asking questions and making summarizing statements. The speaker chooses which path the conversation will follow.

In the last section, Zoey used the listening technique called the "multiple minds theory." Championed by Harvard negotiator David Hoffman, the theory asserts that we all carry around different, often conflicting, emotional states.[6] Unless we vocalize these various states, we won't be able to explain our feelings fully. By walking through each emotional state (angry-self, lonely-self, sixth-grade-immature-self, etc.) we can better understand our range of emotions.

---

5   Renna. S (August 25, 2015) Practicing Presence, Workshop
6   Hoffman, David A. "Mediation, Multiple Minds, and Managing the Negotiation Within." Harv. Negot. L. Rev. 16 (2011): 297.

Becoming a better listener takes effort. It requires discipline, practice, and a genuine interest in others. Great listeners don't have a magical power that others can't learn. Instead, they follow a few simple steps to improve conversations. They get physically prepared before the conversation, ask open-ended questions, and they make listening active, instead of passive.

Prepare Yourself Physically

When listening, we want our body to match our words. A 2010 study by Harvard psychologists showed that we spend roughly forty-seven percent of our waking hours thinking about something other than what we're doing.[7] A wandering mind shows in conversation. Your eyes look around the room, your questions become generalized, and you glance unabashedly at your phone.

Before a conversation begins, kill any potential distractions. Turn off your cell phone and flip it over (your crush is playing the waiting game and so won't text you back for an hour anyways). Physically close your laptop; it's a great demonstration of your focus. Adjust yourself into a comfortable position. Doing so will communicate your willingness to stay for as long as need be. If you are standing, ensure that both of your feet are facing your conversational partner. Creating an "L" with your feet subconsciously communicates a desire to exit a conversation.

---

7   Killingsworth, Matthew A, and Daniel T Gilbert. "A wandering mind is an unhappy mind." Science 330.6006 (2010): 932-932.

Make sure the environment is ripe for listening. If you're in a noisy environment, try to move somewhere else. If you're surrounded by people who will interrupt, move to a more secluded location. Perhaps suggest going for a walk. Room 13 itself provides a good example: the space is isolated, quiet, and distraction free.

Be Encouraging

While comments can unnecessarily alter the flow of a conversation, they remain an important tool to make your partner feel listened to. Stay active as a listener. Give your partner encouraging feedback as they talk by nodding, humming, and saying monosyllabic agreement words such as "yeah," "yup," or "yes." Allow your facial expressions to react to the highs and lows of their story. A practice that is common at Harvard is to snap your fingers in agreement when the person speaking says something you like. While these actions might feel awkward when you first try them, they can be incredibly encouraging to others. Nothing is more soothing for a nervous speaker than a visibly engaged listener.

Listening Practice

Not only should you prepare your environment, but you should also prepare yourself. As with all Cinderella Skills, you can improve through simple practice. Suzanne Renna, a former associate director of Harvard's Bureau of Study Counsel, developed a workshop to invite students to reflect on their style of listening. Part of the workshop is a game, played with partners. If you have a friend nearby, grab them and follow along.

Ask your companion to go first. Have them shut their eyes - feel free to use a blindfold to increase the situational drama.

Meanwhile, you should set an alarm for seven minutes from that time. During those seven minutes, you cannot laugh, make noise, or in any way let your companion know of your presence.

Finally, tell your partner that their mission is to speak for seven minutes. You will sit next to them silently and keep time. After seven minutes of one-sided speaking, the roles will reverse. You will close your eyes to talk while your companion opens their eyes to listen.

At first, this game might feel ridiculous. Why listen for seven minutes without talking? Even more preposterous, how can you talk for seven minutes without any feedback?

What most people find is that the first two to three minutes of speaking are boring. People mostly give a soliloquy composed of small talk. "My classes are great. I hate snow. Man, this game sure is weird. Haha. Ha. ha."

But, after the three minute mark, the conversation begins to change; people run out of obvious things to say. Speakers could choose to sit in silence, but most start to follow tangents they didn't expect. After seven minutes, people have told life-stories, tried to work through a problem, or shared a little insecurity that had been nagging at their mind. Not every speech cuts deep, but participants are often surprised at the strange directions their free-flowing mind goes. Many comment that they feel like they learned more in a pair of seven-minute speeches than they would have in a thirty-minute back and forth conversation.

The listening game reveals that listeners influence a conversation more than we think. When someone speaks freely, they follow the conversation path they'd like to take. Every time a listener asks a question, makes a supportive noise, or adds their perspective, the conversation shifts - sometimes away from what the speaker had wanted to say.

In real interactions, don't sit silently, stifle laughter, or blindfold your companion. Rather, keep in mind how your words, expressions, and presence influence the path of a conversation. Before asking a question, reflect. Is this question for your sake or theirs? If it's only for you, consider holding back to let the other side speak.

Active Listening

When you do have to speak, try active listening. When there is a pause in the conversation, summarize what you heard and repeat it back to your partner. If your friend complains at lunch that their quantum mechanics class is hard, do not reply "No shit." Rather, say something like, "It sounds like quantum is an unbelievably challenging class; props to you for being brave enough to take it on." When your lunch friend hears you summarizing their problem, they'll subconsciously understand that you're listening. This will help deepen your connection and allow the conversation to progress. Active listening works better than you might think. Here's an example conversation.

> Partner: *"Man, I'm really having a hard time with Richard Branson. He's constantly complaining that we don't spend enough time together."*
>
> You: *"Oof. It sounds like he's asking a lot of you, is that right?"*
>
> Partner: *"Yeah, it is! It's like whatever I do isn't enough for him..."*

A good rule of thumb is to end paraphrasing by asking if you have it right, or if they could correct you to help you understand. When people are misunderstood, they can feel frustrated and lonely. If you instead offer that you might be wrong, you give your partner an easier path to politely correct your assumptions.

Like any skill, active listening can be overused. As the philosopher Jiddu Krishnamurti put it, "When you (listen) to somebody... then you are listening not only to the words but also to the feeling of what is being conveyed, to the whole of it, not part of it." Approach paraphrasing as a tool. If it helps you understand your partner, great. If it distracts you from the conversation, relax and try something new.

ASK GREAT QUESTIONS

At some point, you will need to intervene in the conversation. Sometimes the dialogue is shallow and could benefit from more depth. Sometimes a topic is dry, so you need to move to something new. Sometimes your partner has a Spongebob Squarepants tattoo. In each case, you should probably ask a question.

Here's a small example, of a not-so-great-question. Imagine that your friend came to you with a school-related problem. Partner: "Quantum physics has been hard recently. To be honest, I don't like the math we're forced to do."

It would be easy for you to ask a simple "yes" and "no" question. Don't - such a question has the potential to end the conversation. Here's an example of this perilous trap.

You: "So, you don't like math?"

Partner: "Nope."

You: (*begins searching for exit to conversation*)

Avoid this. When you ask questions, try to keep them open-ended. Doing so has a similar effect to pausing - it allows the speaker to direct the conversation. One of the best open ended questions is "Why?"

We did not pioneer this word - children did. Young souls are amazing at breaking down ideas by repeatedly asking "Why?" It is such an effective strategy that Toyota Motor Company developed a similar style of questioning for their manufacturing process.[8] Through their "Five Whys" rule, they attempted to get to the root of any issue. Here's an example from a broken car.

Why? - The battery is dead.

Why? - The alternator is not functioning.

Why? - The alternator belt has broken.

Why? - The alternator belt was well beyond its useful service life and was not replaced.

Why? - The vehicle was not maintained according to the recommended service schedule.

Now let's consider how it might play out if you were to ask your partner, "Why?"

Why? - Because math is pretty tedious I guess, it's always taken me longer than others to finish the problems.

Why? - Because I had a pretty tough time learning the basics back in highschool to be honest.

...Why? - Well... I guess my parents were never around that often to push me to complete the assignments before going out with friends.

Why? - Um, I think they worked too hard. Two careers meant less focus on their only child, me.

Why? - Good question. I guess they felt pressure from society to perform well, and they measured their success in the

---

8   Ohno, Taiichi. Toyota production system: beyond large-scale production. crc Press, 1988.

form of money. I hope I am strong enough to avoid the same mistake.

Why? - Jeez... because society just sucks sometimes? It's just a perpetuating machine that pits people's misguided interests against each other in a giant rat race that is worthless in the end!

...

Why? - God, I don't know! How am I supposed to know the meaning of life? Because some things are, and because some things aren't, okay!? Alright?

Why? - (*partner flees from conversation in an existential crisis*)

This example illustrates two important points. First, if you want to push a conversation past a superficial level simply use the most powerful word in a listener's vocabulary: "why." Second, when used belligerently, "why" can deconstruct a friend into a frightened puddle. We strongly advise not surpassing five "why's" in any one conversation for this reason.

"Why" and similar phrases work well because they can be used in any situation, and cannot be answered with single words. They are verbal tools that allow you to dig deep. Afterwards, it's your choice how to analyze what you find.

Is There Anything Else You'd Like To Say?

Two hours later, Nate, Zoe, and the drop-in were exhausted. Used tissues littered the room. Zoe was massaging her neck. Even the jar of cookies appeared to have dropped a few pounds.

"Is there anything else you'd like to talk about?" Nate asked softly.

The drop-in shook her head no. Instead, she thanked them both quickly and stood up to walk out. The door shut behind her with a concluding click.

Nate and Zoe leaned back into their chairs. Since the drop-in had entered, they'd discussed academic worries, problems with an ex-boyfriend, and even the fear of freshman year ending. Few people can listen for twenty minutes. The counselors had listened for over 120.

And yet, for all they'd been through, the pair was almost euphorically happy. They had listened to someone's story. By being present, they had made that person's life a little better.

If you'd listened, you'd notice that it wasn't a normal conversation. The drop-in told stories that she rarely, if ever, told anyone else. While a pair of counselors had made the conversation special by skillfully listening, if the drop-in hadn't shown bravery, the exchange would have ended unsatisfyingly. By being vulnerable, the drop-in allowed the counselors to help. In her weakness, she'd shown a profound strength.

Vulnerability is power - it's a tenet of Room 13. Following "taking initiative" and "listening," it's the third of our five Cinderella Skills.

TAKE INITIATIVE

LISTEN WELL

BE VULNERABLE

MAKE RITUALS

GIVE OFTEN

5

BE VULNERABLE

"Vulnerability is our most accurate measure of
courage."

- Brené Brown

On the surface, Harvard College student Taylor Carol
looks like a member of a boyband. Straight blond hair crosses
his forehead above his bright blue eyes and charming smile. He
greets you with a handshake and a pat on the back as though you
have been friends for years. He laughs at all of your jokes and
repeats your points to show how much he values your opinion. If
you are not busy trying to be his friend, you are probably trying
to date him. Get in line. He is a talented singer and guitarist,
playing at shows around the country.

Unfortunately, you've never had a long conversation with
Taylor. All you know about him is superficial. You are interested,
but have some early judgments and certainly would not call
yourself his friend. That is, until you find yourself sharing a drink

with him late at night, and you ask him how he got into music. It saved his life, he tells you.

You lower your non-alcoholic drink and lean in. Taylor has all your focus now, and the mood of the conversation has shifted to something much more serious.

When Taylor was eleven, he broke his arm playing baseball. But after weeks of rest, it still didn't heal.[1] The doctors ran blood tests and found his white blood cell count was twenty-five times above normal. Further tests revealed that he had a rare form of leukemia and was promptly diagnosed as terminal.

Facing death at age eleven, he underwent aggressive chemotherapy to put his cancer into remission. Radiation treatment killed his bone marrow, and he spent months in and out of medical isolation. While in the hospital, Taylor was visited by the famous composer Mateo Messina who worked with him on a symphony. After Taylor received a life-saving bone marrow transplant, he and the composer wrote and performed a song. As he recovered more strength, the Make-A-Wish Foundation offered him the opportunity for voice lessons with one of the world's greatest teachers, Seth Riggs. Once recovered at age sixteen - five years after being diagnosed - Taylor dedicated his time to performing at charity events where he helped raise ten million dollars for cancer research. To this day, he still follows his passion for performing music.

He shares with you all of this in a deep and humble manner, cracking jokes at times to lighten the mood while still telling the

---

1 Carol, T. (January 20, 2016) Personal Interview

truth. Others might question his motives for being so vulnerable, but you can tell he's not seeking sympathy. You asked a question, and he simply shared more with you than expected.

When you see him the next day, he smiles brightly and calls you "buddy." Other people make the same superficial judgements about him that you once did, but now you know better. A sense of connection with Taylor motivates you to praise him behind his back. His story may have inspired you, but it was his willingness to share it that strengthened your connection.

VULNERABILITY IS POWER

In 2012, researcher Candice Festa of Loyola University Maryland investigated what predicted the quality of same-sex college friendships.[2] Across one hundred and seventy-six students, sex, class status, extraversion, agreeableness, and interpersonal competencies all influenced the quality of relationships to varying degrees. Surprisingly though, "interpersonal competence of self-disclosure" played a particularly powerful role in predicting friendship quality. Why?

Interpersonal competence of self-disclosure - also known as vulnerability - is powerful because we distrust people who present a "perfect" image. Luckily for you, you aren't perfect. You say the wrong thing, make a mess when you eat, and waste time each day on unreasonably funny cat videos. However, you rarely present this self in social situations.

---

2 Festa, Candice C et al. "Quality Of College Students' Same-Sex Friendships As A Function Of Personality And Interpersonal Competence 1, 2." Psychological reports 110.1 (2012): 283-296.

On the first day of college, you pretend to be flawless. When you talk to a professor, you try to sound confident and worldly. But when sitting alone on your bed calling your high school best friend, it all comes out. You feel overwhelmed by the countless new people and homework assignments. You are unconfident in your choice of clubs and even less confident in your choice of major. Your parents are fighting again, and your love life is limited to the Baywatch poster you plastered on your wall.

You're not alone. Even the strongest characters in fiction, superheroes, are not perfect. Each has a weakness, imaginatively created for a particular purpose: relatability. In psychology, this is called "The Pratfall Effect" (named after the expression for falling on your butt).[3] It describes how people tend to either like or dislike people more after they make an error. When someone we view as average or incompetent makes a mistake, we tend to like them even less. One the flipside, when someone we view as competent makes a mistake, we like them more because it gives us a chance to relate to an individual we admire. In the right situations, weakness can be attractive.

Life is filled with relatable imperfections, but sharing our shortcomings feels scary. Each time Taylor talks about his experience with cancer, he cedes control. Sharing his story risks his friends viewing him differently, as someone to pity instead of admire. We can find this fear in our language itself; the term vulnerable comes from the Latin root "Vulnare," to wound. When we open up to others, we literally feel more open to being

---

3 Aronson, Elliot, Ben Willerman, and Joanne Floyd. "The effect of a pratfall on increasing interpersonal attractiveness." Psychonomic Science 4.6 (1966): 227-228.

hurt. When we act vulnerable, we feel weak. Why does this feeling exist?

According to Texan professor and researcher Brené Brown, the difficulty is rooted in shame.[4] Brown defines shame as pain associated with a fear of disconnection. Would people still accept you if they knew you as well as you know yourself? Perhaps not, you fear.

We all compare ourselves to those around us. But, rather than comparing your full self to another person, you're more likely to compare individual qualities. Abby is better than you in math, Pat is fitter than you, and Sam gets invited to more parties. Regardless of how you compare to any one person holistically, you feel shame for each person that trumps your individual qualities.

All people have things they could share which they choose not to. Sadly, fearful hiding is commonplace and limits opportunities for meaningful connections. Open up. Not only are all people imperfect, but they'll likely share similar imperfections with you. Similarities breed trust and attraction. So, by being vulnerable, we create opportunities for a deeper relationship.

JOHNS LIKE JOANS

To show the importance of similarity, consider the 1985 study by psychologists Richard Kopelman and Dorothy Lang.

4 Brown, Brené. The Power of Vulnerability: Teachings on Authenticity, Connection, & Courage. Sounds True, 2012.

Together their research found a surprising secret to romance: similar names.[5] As their research showed, we are more attracted to people with related names to us. Stephens like Stephanies. Johns like Joans. And Pats? Don't get us started.

This unconscious bias holds true in other fields. In a study of Kiva, a microfinance firm, individuals were more likely to finance projects led by entrepreneurs with similar initials.[6] While there is no evidence that your initials predict your chance of repayment, the study demonstrates a simple truth: we give more trust to people who we are more similar to.

Certain types of similarities - such as matching core values - are even more important for relationships. Lillian Eby of the University of Georgia showed that the single best predictor of a strong mentoring relationship is relatability.[7] Though superficial similarities - such as race, hometown, etc. - helped begin relationships, similar core values best predicted long-term success. In this case, congruency is crucial. As we will discuss later, the more you and your mentor's values align, the better the chance you'll have for a meaningful relationship.

To find deep-level similarities, you need to share frequently, and vulnerably. When Brené Brown studied hundreds of people, a single factor separated those who felt a sense of love and belonging: personal courage. While we now associate "courage"

5 Kopelman, Richard E, and Dorothy Lang. "Alliteration in mate selection: does Barbara marry Barry?." Psychological reports 56.3 (1985): 791-796.

6 Galak, Jeff, Deborah Small, and Andrew T Stephen. "Microfinance decision making: A field study of prosocial lending." Journal of Marketing Research 48.SPL (2011): S130-S137.

7 Eby, Lillian T et al. "Does mentoring matter? A multidisciplinary meta-analysis comparing mentored and non-mentored individuals." Journal of vocational behavior 72.2 (2008): 254-267.

with heroic deeds and valor, the word was historically defined as telling one's mind by telling all one's heart. As we saw with Taylor, revealing your imperfection provides others a chance to connect with you.

How do you become more vulnerable in college? There isn't one perfect strategy. Nonetheless, there are a few areas which we'd like to help you explore. By the end of this section, we'll hope you'll feel comfortable applying vulnerability with professors, significant others, and in situations when emotions run high.

VULNERABILITY WITH PROFESSORS

Consider opening up to a professor. Each teaches tens or hundreds of students a semester. This is in conjunction with the time they spend conducting research and smoking cigars on plush leather chairs (what we assume professors do). From their perspective, most students are just that, pupils in a classroom. Few students take the time to speak with their professors directly. Even fewer share anything meaningful about their personal life.

Opening up to a professor might be more difficult than opening up to a friend, but the benefit can be uniquely valuable. Most professors want to have an influence on the lives of students. Yet, they have few opportunities to do so outside of class. By exposing yourself, you create the opportunity for a meaningful relationship to begin. As we'll explore, it sets the tone for a deeper, more nuanced relationship than one simply between a student and teacher.

The Story Of Adam

Adam, a junior at Harvard, found himself struggling romantically. By his third year of college, he had held four serious relationships. Each ended in tears and a girl claiming Adam was a sociopath. He considered himself a kind, caring partner, but when it came to emotional conflicts he would freeze up and become cruelly cold. He would logically apply every negotiation tactic he knew, such as active listening and speaking about feelings rather than placing blame, but he seemed to be "missing the point."

At the time, Adam was taking a class on negotiation and health policy. He decided to cut his lunch short one Monday and attend office hours for the class. As is common, he was the only student to attend. Professor Daniel Shapiro, Director of the Harvard International Negotiation Initiative, was almost surprised to see that someone had come. He offered a seat and made small talk to ease Adam's nerves.

After a few minutes, Adam asked the question that he had prepared. How could he improve the way he handled emotional conflicts? He shared his past experiences in relationships and even showed the professor a text message from an ex-girlfriend lamenting at his lack of understanding. The professor listened intently and knowingly, nodding and asking interested questions from time to time.

Adam finished his long explanation and asked if the professor knew any applicable research. Professor Shapiro smiled; Adam was in luck. Shapiro had coauthored with Robert Fisher, one of the greatest negotiators of all time, the definitive guide to negotiating around emotions: Beyond Reason.[8] By chance, Adam had shared his interest in something that the professor had been studying for ten years. The intense conversation that followed ran hours over his scheduled time.

From then on, Adam returned each week to continue discussing the same and other deeply personal topics. At one of their final meetings of the semester, the professor asked Adam for help with the release of his new book on negotiation.

Adam would never have encountered such an opportunity had he not been courageous enough to be vulnerable with his professor. Neither him nor his professor would have discovered a similar interest, their conversation would not have become intimate, and their relationship might never have blossomed.

Try following Adam's example. Consider what was spoken about during a course's lecture; find a piece of research that connects with a part of your life; then, during time alone with the professor, mention how their work resonates with you. Of course, this might not be effective for every course - connecting organic chemistry to your last break-up might be difficult - but,

---

8 Fisher, Roger, and Daniel Shapiro. Beyond reason: Using emotions as you negotiate. Penguin, 2005.

you can generally relate an interest of the professor to some facet of your own life.

The professor will likely be touched and excited to have a serious discussion with someone who feels a connection with their work. Don't stop there. Like Adam, use that conversation as a jumping off point. Explore the connection and branch off into other common interests. Through repeated interactions such as office hours or a monthly meeting, continue having difficult conversations. As researchers have found, slowly elevating the amount of self-disclosure is one of the best predictors of a successful relationship.

36 Questions To Fall In Love

In 1997, Dr. Arthur Aron of Stony Brook University wanted to recreate the feeling of love between strangers.[9] In his study, a heterosexual man and woman entered a room. Meeting for the first time, they spent forty-five minutes answering progressively revealing questions. These ranged from the easy, "Would you like to be famous?" to the dangerous, "How do you feel about your relationship with your mother?"

By the end of the study, researchers observed that each pair of subjects had a level of intimacy similar to that of a dating couple. One pair even married six months later and invited the lab to the wedding. Incredibly, researchers had discovered a practical method for developing intimacy.

---

9 Aron, Arthur et al. "The experimental generation of interpersonal closeness: A procedure and some preliminary findings." Personality and Social Psychology Bulletin 23.4 (1997): 363-377.

Nearly twenty years later, the same 36 Questions from the study resurfaced in popular culture with the New York Times Article To Fall In Love With Anyone, Do This. The author, Mandy Len Catron, wrote about asking the questions on a first-date, "I wondered what would come of our interaction. If nothing else, I thought it would make a good story. But I see now that the story isn't about us; it's about what it means to bother to know someone, which is really a story about what it means to be known."[10]

Her story of intentional vulnerability moved millions. Since its publishing, the article has spun off multiple apps, an essay contest, and been shared thousands of times. As Catron remarked, "I think this is the thing that most of us really want… to be known, to be seen, to be understood." By sharing of ourselves, we grow closer to others.

The questions are equally applicable for friends as they are for lovers. The Franklin Fellowship, a tight knit Harvard organization known for the strength of its community, uses the 36 Questions to help new members get to know each other on a deep level. There is potentially no better way to break through a superficial barrier with your roommates than by finding time at night, creating a technology free space, and playing this game. It can also be useful to memorize a few of the questions and ask them in conversations when you would like to uncover a more human side to someone. For your use, we have listed three of the questions below (See the appendix for the complete list).

---

10 "To Fall in Love With Anyone, Do This - The New York Times." 2015. 3 Jun. 2016 <http://www.nytimes.com/2015/01/11/fashion/modern-love-to-fall-in-love-with-anyone-do-this.html>

1. Given the choice of anyone in the world, whom would you want as a dinner guest?

11. Take four minutes and tell your partner your life story in as much detail as possible.

26. Complete this sentence: "I wish I had someone with whom I could share..."

Notice how these questions get progressively more intimate. As researcher Arthur Aron put it, "One key pattern associated with the development of a close relationship among peers is sustained, escalating, reciprocal, personal self-disclosure." In your next conversation, try to use these types of questions as a template. What wouldn't you talk about in a normal conversation? How can you push commonplace chats to that level of intimacy? One thing is for sure, you have to take the first risk.

ACT WITHOUT GUARANTEES

Vulnerability not only involves sharing personal weakness, but also taking on challenges with a risk of failure. According to Brené Brown, vulnerability is basically uncertainty, risk, and emotional exposure. What would happen if you were the first to say "I love you" in a romantic relationship? The first to call someone your best friend?

Kory Floyd, professor of communication at the University of Arizona, decided to measure the effects of verbalizing affection.[11] The participants of the study had an average age of twenty-two years old, similar to the age of college students. The researchers induced heightened levels of stress in the participants in the form of increased blood pressure, heart rate, and levels of the stress hormone cortisol. They were then broken into three groups. One group wrote a letter to a loved one verbalizing their affection. Another sat quietly and thought about people they loved and why they loved them. The final group, as a control, sat and did nothing.

The participants who expressed their affection by writing letters experienced a drastic reduction in stress levels. The stress of the control group remained the same and, interestingly, the thinking group experienced a slight increase in stress hormones.

Stress is both poisonous and ubiquitous in college. Prolonged stress is known to have disastrous health effects including poor sleep quality and decreased cognitive performance. This results in more classroom struggles, which in turn generates more stress. Your relationships suffer as you become noticeably less pleasant to be around. Vocalizing your appreciation of others, and you can reduce some of these effects.

Note that you do not need to be a particularly loving person to experience the benefits of expressing love. Floyd's study asked participants to record how affectionate they considered themselves and found no correlation between their scores and the study results. When you are feeling stressed, simply take the time to write a letter to someone important to you. In it, honestly

11 Floyd, Kory. Communicating affection: Interpersonal behavior and social context. Cambridge University Press, 2006.

express to them how much they mean to you. Not only will you gain a physical boost from doing so, but you will make that person's day.

We often face challenges expressing our emotions - words like "I'm sad," "I'm angry," or "I'm hangry" can feel more limiting than helpful when talking to someone else. The key is giving a balanced assessment of your emotions - combining both the bravery to open up and the self-awareness to know what's within.

UNDERSTANDING YOUR EMOTIONS

You sit at a local diner by yourself, enjoying a lazy afternoon. Your running shoes cast optimistic ambiguity as to whether you will work out today - you won't. The notepad on the table is a hopeful gesture in case you decide to study while eating - you won't. You're trying slightly too hard to catch the eye of the server when your phone buzzes.

You check it to look less lonely. It's your significant other. You two "need to talk." Your remark about their exhaustion the previous night was one passive aggressive comment too many. If you weren't so insensitive, you would have seen that they were stressed because they take harder classes than you - or so they say.

The server notices your tense jaw and clenched fist. He decides to give you a little more time to order.

The server is right, you're furious! Your thumbs move into ready position, prepared to unleash a regrettable text.

Stop.

You are not "angry." What kind of simplistic animal are you to have your vast, indescribable range of feelings squeezed into a single word. Sure, the short-tempered fighter part of you is furious. But the high school debater part of you is really just feeling argumentative. The socially insecure part of you feels hurt and can't take its eyes off the word "insensitive." The cliché romantic part of you already wants to make up by offering a sympathetic hug.

Complex you is full of all these emotional selves and more. But how do you express them? And more fundamentally, should you?

Sharing Emotions

People frequently apologize for their emotions. They probably shouldn't. As psychologist Jonathan M. Adler put it, "Acknowledging the complexity of life may be an especially fruitful path to psychological well-being."[12] In a study on the effect of suppressing feelings, Eric L. Garland of Florida State University and his associates measured the stress increase caused by exposing alcoholics to alcohol based cues. They then compared these physical effects to the subjects measured tendency to suppress emotions. Subjects who were more likely to hold in feelings experienced higher stress responses. The

---

12 "Negative Emotions Are Key to Well-Being - Scientific American." 2014. 3 Jun. 2016 <http://www.scientificamerican.com/article/negative-emotions-key-well-being/>

researchers concluded that sharing an emotion may help you handle it more effectively.[13]

Emotions exist for a reason. They help draw attention to festering health and relationship problems. They help guide your choices and provide feedback as to what truly is important. Avoiding these feelings can feel good in the short-term; who hasn't felt silly after being angry with someone else? However, we want to be clear. You're not stronger by hiding your emotions. You're obscuring a part of yourself from the outside world.

For Taylor, sharing emotions has been particularly painful. As a child in the isolated care unit, he had to watch countless friends die from crippling diseases and invasive procedures. Of the 20+ patients he lived with, he was the only one to survive. Ten years later, he suffers from survivor's guilt. Why did he live when others didn't?

If anyone has reason to shut off from others, it would be Taylor. Yet, he shares openly with the people around him. He understands the value of vulnerability. When he talks about his emotions, he becomes more adept at handling them himself. Even more, he helps other people open up about the difficulties in their own lives.

We all have demons. As college students, we face moments of self-doubt, fear, and guilt. By following Taylor's example, however, we can make reality a little rosier. We can grow stronger

---

13 Garland, Eric L et al. "Thought suppression, impaired regulation of urges, and Addiction-Stroop predict affect-modulated cue-reactivity among alcohol dependent adults." Biological psychology 89.1 (2012): 87-93.

by handling our emotions, and we can make others feel safe enough to share their own.

After Taking Initiative and Listening, Vulnerability is the third, and often most difficult, Cinderella skill. By definition, it involves exposing yourself to pain. Every time you say the words, "I've never told that to anyone before," you hand a small piece of yourself to someone else. They can take it, care for it, and give a piece back. Or they can hurt you.

How do you choose the right person? And, how do you create situations where you can truly be yourself? The truth is, it takes more than one conversation with Taylor to become his friend. You need hundreds of small interactions compiled into one. To make sure you're achieving enough depth in a relationship, we offer one solution: make rituals.

TAKE INITIATIVE

LISTEN WELL

BE VULNERABLE

MAKE RITUALS

GIVE OFTEN

6
MAKE RITUALS

"We are what we repeatedly do. Excellence, then, is not an act, but a habit."

- Aristotle

It was match point.

Morgan bent down, breathing deeply. A small strand of blond hair clung to her forehead. Morgan took her hand off her racquet to brush it from her eyes. Finally, she stood up to serve.

Whack.

The squash ball pounded against the wall. Her opponent dived to retrieve it. The rally had begun.

Hit after hit bounced around the court. Morgan hit a low volley; her opponent countered with a light lob. Morgan drove the ball across the left wall. Her opponent returned the ball cross-court. Finally, Morgan saw an opening. She hit the ball at the corner of the court. Her opponent, caught on the other side, would need to sprint to return it.

Her opponent charged and swung wildly for the hit.

His body collided with Morgan's.

The ball dropped to the ground, untouched.

Morgan crumpled to the floor, unconscious.

The following five minutes for Morgan were a blur.[1] She recalls standing back up with a pounding headache. The strand of hair had fallen back over her eyes. But, she couldn't see it. She only saw a shimmering white wall in front of her.

Then suddenly, her hearing returned.

The world rang like a 50s era telephone. Little by little, she heard her coach shouting her name. "Morgan… Morgan… Are you okay? Are you alright?"

Morgan waved her coach off. She was fine. The referee had called the collision a "let." They'd have to replay the point.

Morgan served again - an ace. The game was over. She shook her opponent's hand and walked back to the stands to grab her phone. Immediately, she called for help.

"Mom, I think I need a doctor."

The doctor's diagnosis was serious, but not surprising. The hit to Morgan's head had caused a concussion. She should stay in bed for the next few days, and within a week she should feel better.

---

1   Breitmeyer, M. (January 3, 2016) Personal Interview

As Morgan returned to her house, she knew something didn't feel right. She'd had a concussion before, but it hadn't felt like this. Still, Morgan hoped the doctor was right. So, she went back home and slept.

For the next few days, Morgan could barely function. She could talk, but only in spurts. She could eat, but only in doses. Loud noises hurt and bright lights were unbearable.

A few days later, she returned to the doctor. The diagnosis was the same. Go back home and rest for a few days. You'll return to normal soon.

But she didn't. Morgan tried to go back to school the next day. By the end of the twenty-minute bus ride, she was crying in pain. She returned to the doctor for the third time.

This time, the doctor ordered an MRI brain scan. As she glanced over the results, he gave Morgan a worried glance. The injury wasn't a concussion. Instead, Morgan's brain had suffered three independent strokes.

On that fateful day, the trajectory of Morgan's life changed forever. As the doctor explained, Morgan might never function at the same level again. Her future with squash was over. Even her ability to read, write, or think might never return to previous levels. She should go home and rest; only time would tell.

And yet, five years later, it's hard to recognize Morgan as that injured high school girl. Since her diagnosis, she was recruited by Stanford to play squash, she was elected vice-president of her high school class, and she ultimately decided to attend Harvard to study math.

How did she recover? Part of the answer lies in the small, seemingly insignificant rituals she created. Indeed, Morgan has a power that goes beyond squash, math, or student government; she knows how to create habits and stick with them.

To understand how Morgan thrived despite her injury, we need to step back and learn how habits are formed, the power of the mere exposure effect in social settings, and why trying out new restaurants can be a bad idea.

How Do You Develop Habits That Stick?

Motivation and willpower poorly predict a long-term habit's success. As the founder of the Stanford Persuasive Technology Lab argues, "Motivation relates to… temporary behavioral change (but not long-term change)."[2] If you rely primarily on motivation, you're using a losing strategy. How you develop habits is more important than your desire for the habit to stick.

So, how should we make new habits? According to author of The Power of Habit, Charles Duhigg, we first need to understand what habits are. A habit is a routine behavior that is repeated regularly and often unconsciously. Each consists of three main parts: a cue, a routine, and a reward. A cue is a mental primer that tells you to start the habit. Arriving home after work might

---

2   Fogg, Brian J. "A behavior model for persuasive design." Proceedings of the 4th international Conference on Persuasive Technology 26 Apr. 2009: 40.

be a cue for some people to grab a snack. A routine is the habit itself; for example, eating the snack. Finally, the reward is the psychological benefit of doing the habit. Perhaps it's a feeling of fullness, or maybe it's simply taking a break after work.[3]

Imagine, for example, you're trying to develop a habit of eating cheesecake once a week with a friend. You two have tried to make the habit before, but you've consistently failed. Either you're both too busy or you couldn't find cheesecake in a timely manner.

The first step is creating a consistent cue. You are guaranteed to already have a number of daily traditions (a life without any habits is almost too extreme to imagine). These could range from brushing your teeth, to eating dinner, to procrastinating real work. Regardless of what they are, your traditions all begin with a primer - something that subconsciously reminds you to begin the habit. A cue could be time related, but it also could be locational or situational.

Based on this idea of reminders, you decide to have the weekly cheesecake on Wednesdays at 4:00 PM with your friend. The midweek boredom combined with afternoon cravings will serve as your cue.

Once the cue occurs, the routine starts. This is easy, you stuff your face with dessert while your friend unloads their problems.

---

3   Duhigg, Charles. The power of habit: Why we do what we do in life and business. Random House, 2012.

Lastly, you need a reward for being such a good weekly friend. This reward is crucial because it reinforces the habit overtime. While we often think rewards need to be large, a reward simply needs to indicate completion.

For illustration, think about toothpaste. Have you ever felt that tingly, minty-fresh feeling after brushing your teeth? That feeling is your "reward" at the end of brushing. It's a small reminder that you've completed the habit successfully. Interestingly, the cleaning chemicals in toothpaste don't naturally give a tingly sensation. Instead, toothpaste companies have added chemicals like citric acid or mint oil to create the feeling. Overtime, your brain starts to crave the tingle, motivating you to brush your teeth daily. For your cheesecake expedition, your reward could be the sugar high you get from the encounter. But, if that's not enough, grab a mint on the way out of the café, so you too can enjoy some minty fresh validation. Go on champ, you deserve it.

As Aristotle once said, "We become what we repeatedly do." Getting habits right in college is important. But can we take this concept further? Few people have mastered repetition and commitment to the extent that Morgan has. But, before she could create those traditions, she needed to do something more basic: eat, sleep, and create new friends after eighteen months away.

THE PATH TO RECOVERY

Before her injury, Morgan was the model of a successful high school student. She was one of the top mathematics students in the nation, served as a representative on the Boston youth city council, and was so talented at squash that she played for her high school's boys team.

But, for the next six months, Morgan was none of those things. Her ability to concentrate disappeared, making math problems painful instead of fun. Her short-term memory began to fail, making it impossible to attend youth city council meetings. For days at a time, she wouldn't leave the bed, much less play squash.

After six months of healing, Morgan began to add small challenges to her day. As she said, "It was a routine. Each day, I'd try to do one thing. Sometimes, I'd do a single math problem. Other times, I'd read a page of a book." The road to recovery was arduous. But, almost imperceptibly, Morgan began to improve.

After eighteen months, she returned to play squash.

Physically, Morgan looked the same as before. She was sixteen, tall, and athletic. Her blond hair still fell over her eyes as she talked.

In other ways, Morgan's life couldn't return to normal. For the last six months, she'd added schoolwork in small doses at a time. But, after every few hours, she still needed to rest. Her old high school refused to accommodate her new learning needs. So, she began to study online and at home.

While academics improved, her friendships still suffered from the time off. After a year and a half away, classmates from high school had moved on. Because she studied at home, she would only see them if they planned to meet up. She easily relearned how to serve a squash ball, but she couldn't easily reconnect with former friends.

Flash forward two years, and you'd see a completely different Morgan; the Morgan you'd see would be surrounded by close friends, a prom date, and powerful mentoring relationships. How did Morgan go from feeling lonely to feeling loved? She capitalized on one of the most powerful effects in psychology: mere exposure.

The Mere Exposure Effect

On February 27, 1967, the Associated Press released a story about a peculiar class:

"A mysterious student has been attending a class at Oregon State University for the past two months enveloped in a big black bag. Only his bare feet show. Each Monday, Wednesday, and Friday at 11:00 A.M. the Black Bag sits on a small table near the back of the classroom. The class is Speech 113— basic persuasion. . . . Charles Goetzinger, professor of the class, knows the identity of the person inside. None of the twenty students in the class do. Initially the students were wary of the black bag. Goetzinger said the students' attitude changed

from hostility toward the Black Bag to curiosity and finally to friendship."[4]

The professor, Charles Goetzinger, brought in the hooded student to prove a point: we like what we repeatedly see. Given enough time, fear of an unknown is replaced with affection for the common. The first time you pick up a razor to shave your proud facial patchwork, you hold it gingerly out of fear of cutting yourself. After a year you wield your bathroom Excalibur with ease and carelessness. In social psychology, this phenomenon is called the "mere exposure effect," and it holds true for almost anything. Simply put, the more we interact with something, the more we like it.

In 1968, psychologist Robert Zajonc tested the relationship between exposure and attitude towards nonsense words. In a famous experiment, researchers generated a list of twelve "Turkish" words including "Ikitaf", "Enanwal", and "Dilikli." In reality, all twelve words were randomly invented for the experiment.

The researchers showed groups of students the words while pronouncing them and having the students verbally repeat. In each group, the experimenter changed how many times the subject repeated the word. To finish, researchers asked the students to rate the "goodness" of each word.

Exposure equaled liking. The more times researcher showed a word, the higher students rated the word's "goodness." This

4   Zajonc, Robert B. "Attitudinal effects of mere exposure." Journal of personality and social psychology 9.2p2 (1968): 1.

effect held true for Chinese characters, advertisements, and photos of others. The mere exposure effect is one of the most robust effects in all of social psychology.

In college, it's easy to meet new people. You have new classes each semester; you move dorms every year; you even bump into people in the caféteria salad bar. On the other hand, college - unlike high school - makes it difficult to see the same people. There are no school wide assemblies, fewer mandatory classes, and no consistent lunchtime. Besides your roommates, there are few people in a university you have to see regularly.

Creative habits help you spend time with another person. Perhaps you workout together five mornings a week, do the laundry every Sunday morning, or talk before going to bed on weekends. The actual activity is nearly irrelevant as long as it is consistent.

Be deliberate with how you spend your social time. Rituals can often be activities done with other people. But as we will see, they can also be a place that you try to go often.

Why You Shouldn't Try That New Café

In 1950, MIT researchers began to study the effect of physical distance on friendship. The team began by finding a dorm on campus - Westgate. They then tracked the lives of dozens of students within the dorm. The researchers were intrigued by the factors that led to friendship. Earlier research had already shown that similar values, interests, and physical appearance resulted in friendship. But, was there anything else?

Through their analysis, the MIT team found that physical proximity was the single biggest predictor of friendship.[5] Random encounters with people in the hallway, common room, or attempts to secretly steal the communal shampoo, added up to create genuine relationships. When students were asked to list their closest friends, they often did just that; they listed the friends who lived physically closest to them.

The researchers expected location to affect friendship, but they didn't realize how large that effect would be. Controlling for various other factors, students were ten times more likely to become friends with someone in their building than with someone in another building. They were more likely to have friends who lived on the same floor, and were even more likely to become friends with next door neighbors rather than people who lived down the hallway. In a college of 5000 students, physical proximity was found to matter more to relationships than religious affiliation, similarity of interest, or place of origin.

Think back to your life and you'll notice the effect. How many of your childhood friends lived nearby? How close are you to your next-door neighbor? What about the neighbor three houses away? In many cases, we feel relationships are serendipitous. Your best friend and you "happened" to sit next to each other in math. But, the causality is often the opposite - you grew close to each other because you had the opportunities to

---

5   Festinger, Leon, Kurt W Back, and Stanley Schachter. Social pressures in informal groups: A study of human factors in housing. Stanford University Press, 1950.

Your Relationship GPA

repeatedly interact. Proximity is the most powerful, and often least thought about, factor in everyday relationships.

Be deliberate about the places you frequent. Take cafés, for example. Similar to meeting new people during your first months of college, it is worth spending your time in a new environment exploring all nearby coffee shops. After testing a wide breadth of locations, experiment committing to just one. Over time, you'll notice how you recognize others. If you take initiative, fellow regulars can quickly become friends.

One of Morgan's best friends, Stephen, spent his freshman summer living in Rwanda. While he was there, he decided to experiment with the concept of propinquity. So, he chose one coffee shop and worked there the entire summer. He wrote about it in his personal blog, which we've excerpted from below.

Home is where embraces last a little too long. And, as my shirt mingles with the sweaty remains of Daniel Gasangwa's hug, I feel it. This has become home.

Today is my final day in Rwanda and I'm writing from a place called the Klab. For reference, the Klab is an innovation center here in Kigali, Rwanda. It provides an open space for tech-entrepreneurs to collaborate and work on IT related products. It is free, wifi-intensive, and over the past eight weeks has become my home-away-from-home.

And even though today is my final day here, it hasn't been too different from others. I arrived early, butchered a couple of handshakes with friends, and exchanged an English-

Kinyarwanda lesson with Fais – the barista. (She taught me "to be happy," I taught her "Jeggings," "Parmesan," and "Kerfuffle.")

No, today hasn't been too different from any other; but because it is the last, I've started to reminisce on how this total-nerd-center became my Rwandan abode.

I started going to the Klab out of necessity. I needed a place to program, to write in my blog, and to respond to the increasingly frantic facebook statuses from my mom. The Klab was close, free, and beautiful. And the more I went, the more I saw the same people. I made friends, found a favorite chair, and even began low-level Kinyarwanda banter with the guards: "Good afternoon," "good afternoon to YOU." (I leave.)

By about the third week in Rwanda, however, I realized that there were a number of other Wifi-rich places near my house (A café, library, etc.)

Which led to a new dilemma: should I explore those other places? Or should I continue going to the Klab?

Now, I think that the travel buff inside me would argue that we should always explore new places – I mean, why else travel but to explore? And yet this time I consciously decided not to. Instead of trying new places, I would stick with one that I liked and see it through till my final day.

Today is that day and as I overhear Fais murmuring "Kerfuffle" to herself, I realize I feel something here that I've never felt while traveling – real belonging.

And I think the base reason is that I made myself explore less. In the time when I could have seen other places, I instead came back to the Klab. In doing so, I made friends and a small home... [6]

Stephen's revelation to build a ritual around a café wasn't original. Morgan had done something similar years before. Her ritual allowed her access to relationships she would have never otherwise formed, and mentors who guided her on her path to recovery.

SMALL STEPS AND OLD MEN

Instead of lamenting her loss of friends, Morgan decided to create new rituals outside of school. Every day, she'd wake up and practice squash for two hours. Then she'd take an online class, nap, and finish her homework. She found a rhythm in rituals, the most powerful of which being a weekly Friday dinner.

"Each Friday, my Mom and I would eat dinner at the squash club. We'd sit at the bar and talk with the same group of old men." And, as Morgan returned each Friday, she became a quasi-daughter to each of them. "They'd talk to me about politics, business, and problems with their wives. It was weird being a sixteen-year-old with seventy-year-old friends. But, it was also fun."

For the next two years, this group of men stayed constant in Morgan's life. They asked her to babysit their children, played

6   "5 Reasons You Should Explore LESS While ... - Stephen Turban." 2014. 4 Jun. 2016 <http://www.stephenturban.com/5-reasons-you-should-explore-less-while-traveling-abroad/>

squash with her in the mornings, and mentored her as she applied to college. With the group as support, she returned to an almost "normal" life. She graduated top of her class in her online high school, became senior class vice-president, and even flew out to California for her online high school's prom. (You think your prom was awkward? Try having never met your date). Torn between schools recruiting her for her academic skills, squash performance, and prom-dance-floor-moves, Morgan ultimately chose Harvard.

Once Morgan entered college, she would face one of her life's greatest challenges - freshman year friends. Like all students, she needed to choose between a few deep friends and a broader network of weaker connections. Once again, Morgan used rituals to balance between the broad and the deep.

THE DIFFERENCE BETWEEN BREADTHWORKING AND DEPTHWORKING

In the late 1990s, researcher B.T. McWhirter investigated loneliness in college students. While he predicted that a high percentage of them combated social isolation on a regular basis, after interviewing over 625 students his results still shocked him. Over thirty percent of students reported feeling lonely at some time. More than five percent saw it as a major problem in their life.[7]

---

7   McWhirter, Benedict T. "Loneliness, learned resourcefulness, and self-esteem in college students." Journal of Counseling & Development 75.6 (1997): 460-469.

Entering college is difficult for everyone. For perhaps the first time, you're coming into an environment where you know almost no one. As a result, you search blindly for friends. You make your first connections based on temporary circumstances such as orientation programs, and superficial commonalities like hometowns - useful factors when bonding with new people, but not necessarily the best predictors of long lasting relationships.

After a few months of school, you likely feel like you've developed a few friends. You walk into a dining hall and recognize faces. As you move through campus, you wave at a few people. You might even be invited to a party.

But, while the number of your relationships grow, their depth might not. As Andrew Kim, Harvard class of 2015 wrote, "Despite the vast number of superficial connections... truly satisfying relationships are incredibly difficult to achieve. Even the very people who seem to thrive can suffer from a lack of a deep, nourishing bond with another human being."[8]

By the end of the first semester of freshman year, you face a challenge. You may have more "friends" than ever, but, you trust only a handful of people - if any. You wonder if your friendships will ever feel as comfortable and warm as they did in high school.

Like all things in life, it is important to have a balance between acquaintances and trusted connections. Broad social networks often receive the bulk of attention and respect, and that is not necessarily a bad thing. In fact, over the past decade there

---

8   "Lonely at Harvard? | Opinion | The Harvard Crimson." 2014. 4 Jun. 2016 <http://www.thecrimson.com/article/2014/1/28/harvard-lonely-at-harvard/>

has been much investigation to understand the importance of networking. As research from Harvard Business School professor Francesca Gino showed, lawyers who networked the most frequently had the most billable hours.[9] The same holds true for students. The broader your network, the more opportunities you'll have. Some individuals are talented at building broad networks. We call them "Breadthworkers."

Others, however, are stronger at building deep, meaningful connections. They might not have as many friends. But, the friends they do have are endlessly loyal and loving. We'll call these people "Depthworkers." Depthworkers understand how rituals can bridge the gap between the fleeting faces of freshman year and the secure friendships of graduation. Both breadthworking and depthworking are important for your Relationship GPA. But, for some students, meeting new people isn't the challenge - nor is building deep friendships. For Morgan, the challenge was a broken bone.

ARE RITUALS STRONGER THAN YOUR BODY?

Days before college began, Morgan was forced to return to the doctor. Her hip had been hurting her throughout the summer. She'd seen a personal trainer. She'd spoken with a chiropractor. But, nothing seemed to help. Again, the doctors took an x-ray.

---

9   "Professional Networking Makes People Feel Dirty - HBS Working ..." 2015. 4 Jun. 2016 <http://hbswk.hbs.edu/item/professional-networking-makes-people-feel-dirty>

She had broken her hip. Only four days before her freshman year, Morgan took up crutches. For the second time in her life, doctors told her she'd never play squash again.

Most freshmen feel lost during their first few weeks. Morgan didn't just feel lost; she felt defeated.

As she tells it, "Some people enter college and they have this community. Perhaps it's their sports team or their religion. But, after I lost squash, I wasn't sure what that was for me. I started asking who was I other than that?"

For the first year of college, Morgan faced the common freshman challenge of too many acquaintances and too few deep friendships. As she puts it, "I had a lot of friends, but I wasn't very close with most of them." But, unlike most students, Morgan already knew how to change this. She needed to create traditions with the friends that mattered most to her.

During the freshman year at Harvard, all students live in a central campus called "Harvard Yard." Once students start their second year, they enter an upperclassmen "house." Each house has 300 to 400 students who live, eat, and spend most of their time there. The houses are more spread out over campus than Harvard Yard. Though students meet new people in their house, they often lose their early friendships from freshman year.

For Morgan, losing these friends wasn't an option. Inspired by her time in the squash club, she brainstormed potential rituals. Creating a tradition communicated that she cared. "Once you leave freshman year, you don't see them every day. But if you establish a tradition with them, you tell them you're important to me."

First, Morgan approached a friend who was living in a house that was particularly far away. She asked to have lunch once a week on Monday. Her friend, excited to escape her geographical isolation, agreed enthusiastically. Morgan next approached another of her closest friends. She again asked to create a tradition: two meals a week, one dinner and one lunch. Again, her friend agreed happily.

As the rituals continued, Morgan's friendships grew deeper. If a different friend asked to have a meal during one of those times, she'd politely decline. Then she'd offer another time that didn't conflict with her traditions. As we'll discuss later, Morgan intuitively did two things: she prioritized and ritualized. As she did, she built some of the deepest connections of her life.

Many people leave college without ever developing a lifetime friendship. But, for Morgan, the solution lies in making a commitment. "I think at Harvard people are so busy, that unless you become part of their routine… it's hard to track them down. If you commit one hour every week, then they feel like they can do the same."

Some people avoid ritual because they feel like it's a waste of time. But, these people misunderstand something fundamental about life: there isn't a tension between friendship and success. Rather, the two are inexorably linked.

Despite a lifetime of challenge, Morgan is one of the most successful students at Harvard. She worked for a hedge fund her sophomore summer. She teaches statistics courses to graduate students. She's even president of a female social club at Harvard - a high honor. Most importantly, Morgan has friends who love her. As Morgan commits to others, people commit to her. Her focus on creating loyal traditions has helped her balance having a broad spread of friends, with having a few number of deeply invested relationships. To show her loyalty, encourage commitment from her friends, and build an unbreakable trust, Morgan follows the most important tenet of rituals: consistency.

THE IMPORTANCE OF CONSISTENCY: THE 100% RULE

Traditions sound great in theory. But traditions are founded on doing something consistently. As you and your New Year's resolutions know, staying on track is difficult.

Imagine, you choose a local café as "your place." Great. You go there regularly. You expertly navigate their overly specific menu. The barista calls you "hun." You love it.

Now imagine that a friend tells you about another café. The atmosphere is retro, the baristas are pretty, and the spice chai? The spiciest.

You're tempted. The grass looks greener on the other side. But, you've also made a commitment to your current place. So, what do you do?

Let's try a different example. Imagine now, you have a weekly lunch date with a friend. but you just learned a famous speaker is on campus. You've heard great things about her, though missing your weekly lunch would break your ritual.

What do you do?

In both cases, it seems reasonable to break tradition. After all, it's not like you're cheating on a café. Your friend is probably fine with changing the lunch time. In both cases, you can return to your routine after the exception.

Or, at least you think you can. As HBS professor Clayton Christensen argues, it is easier to follow your values all of the time rather than most of the time. As he said, "Decide what you stand for, then stand for it all the time. It's easier to hold your principles 100 percent of the time than it is to hold them ninety-eight percent of the time."[10]

Christensen calls "just-this-once" thinking "the trap of marginal thinking." Just as you know that rabbit-based food preferences are good for your long term health, companies know that long term investments are good. But all too frequently, both you and companies fall into the fallacy that you can afford to be shortsighted "just this once."

Blockbuster illustrates the trap of marginal thinking perfectly. In the 1990's, Blockbuster was the largest source of home-video in the nation. They had billions in assets and

---

10   Christensen, Clayton M, James Allworth, and Karen Dillon. How will you measure your life?. HarperBusiness, 2012.

thousands of employees. By 1993, there were more than 3400 stores making them the most powerful brand in the market.

In the late 1990s, a small company called Netflix joined the DVD market. Their idea was simple. Instead of making people go to the video store, they would send DVDs in the mail.

By the early 2000s, the Netflix business model showed promise. They'd earned $150 million in revenue and had a thirty-six percent profit margin. It had become clear that the current Blockbuster model wouldn't last much longer. As the Chicago Sun-Times wrote, "Imagine a Blockbuster night without Blockbuster, (a time when no video store will ever slap you with a late fee or fine you for failing to rewind.) Because in this world, there are no videos, only home computers."[11]

Netflix's business model was the future, but Blockbuster could have copied it easily. If Blockbuster had chosen to develop their own DVD home-delivery, they would have surely done well. They had a stronger brand and financial backing. Yet, Blockbuster didn't add DVD delivery until 2004 - already too late. By 2011, Netflix had twenty-four million customers. Blockbuster had declared bankruptcy the year before.

11   "Blockbuster's Rise and Fall: The Long, Rewinding Road - TheStreet." 2016. 6 Jun. 2016 <https://www.thestreet.com/story/10867574/4/the-rise-and-fall-of-blockbuster-the-long-rewinding-road.html>

WHAT WENT WRONG WITH BLOCKBUSTER?

Blockbuster made decisions with the economic principle "marginal analysis." Marginal analysis is looking at that bite of cheesecake and weighting the bliss you'll achieve from eating it against the hundreds of grams of sugar saturated deep in its creamy depths. In economic terms, it's the analysis of the additional benefits of an activity compared to the additional costs. In theory, choices based on marginal differences should be great. You would stop exactly when you need to. But, in practice, marginal analysis leads you down a long path of sugary mistakes.

Part of the problem is that humans are terrible at judging the future. We buy a gym membership certain that we'll have motivation; but when we wake up in the morning, we'd rather sleep an extra hour than develop our chiseled calves. In economics, this is called "temporal discounting." It's the idea that people value things differently for different time horizons.

We tend to overinflate current gains and underestimate future costs. At college, you value a pumpkin spiced latte now more than one you can have in a month. Paying back money in a month appears not as costly as spending money now. So, on your way to your 8:00 AM lecture, you swipe your credit card at Starbucks before running to class, slightly more in debt than when you woke up.

Blockbuster was no better than 8:00 AM you. When Blockbuster looked at the new type of DVD market, they misvalued the benefits and costs. In the near-term, they saw a steep price. They'd have to create a new distribution network. Even worse, they wouldn't be able to use their biggest resource: their stores. The marginal cost of new investment was greater than the short run benefit that it would bring. So, they didn't adapt.[12] Unfortunately, this mistake led to Blockbuster's fall.

Marginal-cost and temporal discounting help us better understand our choices around tradition. At any point, there will be dozen of opportunities to break ritual. On the margin, the cost of reneging on a tradition feels small, but overtime these small breaks add up. Together, they form the big picture of your life.

Defeating Marginal Thinking

How do you overcome "marginal thinking?" Create a tradition. Then follow it 100% of the time.

To some, this might sound overzealous. Being consistent with traditions makes sense, but what about when something comes up? Shouldn't everyone be a little flexible? The person you share a tradition with would understand - they break their commitments all the time!

Unfortunately, flexibility leads to complication and cost. As Professor Eldar Schaffer and Sendhir Mullainathan argue in their book Scarcity: Why Having Too Little Means So Much, simplicity is vital. They argue that the amount of mental

---

12   Christensen, Clayton M, James Allworth, and Karen Dillon. How will you measure your life?. HarperBusiness, 2012.

space you have should be conserved. When you have more "bandwidth," you make better decisions. Deciding when to be flexible with your rituals and when not to be, causes you to waste mental energy which leads to worse decisions.[13]

In a study found in the Journal of Consumer Research, researchers showed that dieters with a taxed bandwidth were less able to resist cravings. Unfortunately, they also showed that being on a diet decreased your mental bandwidth. The constant pressure of eating the right amount, expended significant mental energy. This created a catch-22. You needed bandwidth to avoid cravings. But, to avoid cravings, you needed to use the same mental energy.[14]

The best way to avoid the mental tax was to reduce complexity.[15] So, instead of counting calories, complete bans on certain types of food proved more effective. For example, completely cutting out carbs was easier to process than limiting carbs to two servings for a meal. The simplicity reduced unneeded decision making, and in the long run, it improved adherence to the diet.

The same is true for traditions. For most students, the difficulty isn't believing traditions are healthy. Rather, it's executing long-term. Counterintuitively, the best way to make

13   Mullainathan, Sendhil, and Eldar Shafir. Scarcity: Why having too little means so much. Macmillan, 2013.

14   Shiv, Baba, and Alexander Fedorikhin. "Heart and mind in conflict: The interplay of affect and cognition in consumer decision making." Journal of consumer Research 26.3 (1999): 278-292.

15   Mata, Jutta, Peter M Todd, and Sonia Lippke. "When weight management lasts. Lower perceived rule complexity increases adherence." Appetite 54.1 (2010): 37-43.

sure a tradition lasts is through inflexibility. Commit to a time or place. Then only change it after long-term reflection.

STARTING A TRADITION

The Grant Study of 268 Harvard sophomores highlighted the importance of relationships. But friendships only deepen if you deliberately invest time in them. To do this, you need to spend time consistently with the ones you love. Some say the "grass is greener on the other side." We argue instead, "The grass is greenest where you water it."

The easiest shared rituals are founded in your weird quirks. If, for example, you and a friend have a love of a unique food, make sure to eat it together. Morgan and her best friend have a bi-weekly vegetarian meal. Both of them adore veggies - to an alienating degree; so, their meal is the perfect opportunity for them to share a rare love. After years of practice, they have yet to miss a single meal.

Routinely sharing a meal comes with added perks. According to a study in the journal of Human Performance by food scientists at Cornell, when employees eat together their cooperation and work performance increase.[16] Other studies have shown that eating family meals is correlated to positive physical and mental health.[17] While you may not have coworkers

---

16   Kniffin, Kevin M et al. "Eating Together at the Firehouse: How workplace commensality relates to the performance of firefighters." Human Performance 28.4 (2015): 281-306.

17   Utter, Jennifer et al. "Relationships between frequency of family meals, BMI and nutritional aspects of the home food environment among New Zealand adolescents." International Journal of Behavioral Nutrition and Physical Activity 5.1 (2008): 50.

or family at college, eating with classmates and friends can reproduce these same benefits.

Now, not all rituals have to be based around food. You can work out, watch a TV show, host a party, learn how to make a new cocktail, take photos, go shopping, play music, drink tea, or even write a book... Think of any favorite pastime you have. Chances are you can make it a ritual with a friend.

In a world of constant opportunity, traditions keep you focused. They help you prioritize those who matter. And, perhaps most importantly, they let you meet seventy year-old squash players. (Or maybe that's just Morgan.)

But, how do you show your commitment to someone you just met? You help them out. As we'll show in the next chapter, giving to others is the difference between good and bad medical students, it's the reason you do or don't receive a call back interview, and it's the root of one Rhodes Scholar's success.

TAKE INITIATIVE

LISTEN WELL

BE VULNERABLE

MAKE RITUALS

GIVE OFTEN

7

GIVE OFTEN

"No one is useless in this world who lightens the burdens of another."

- Charles Dickens

You meet Neil Alacha in a coffee shop. He arrives before you, already sipping on a 16 oz. mug of coffee. It's his fourth. You'd think for a man who consumes 500 mg of caffeine a day, he'd be a bit more twitchy. As he sees you arrive, he smoothly waves and invites you to sit.

Neil takes a drink of coffee. Then he asks, "How are you?"

Typically, that particular question feels hollow, similar to a perfunctory "hello," "what's up," or "what's new." But, when Neil asks it, there's a certain weight. As if by answering "fine" or "good" you'd disappoint both him and yourself. The way Neil gazes patiently across the table makes you want to share. So, you do.

Neil takes another sip.

Thirty minutes later, you awaken to find yourself talking about your love of a Korean anime TV show. Looking up, you realize Neil's been listening intently the entire time. Occasionally, he had asked questions, or made sounds of agreement. But, for the most part, he'd sat appreciating your story. You just spoke non-stop for half an hour. Not only that, but you feel cared for, listened to, and known.

The myth of Neil Alacha is real.

Neil is something of a legend at Harvard College. Over the past four years, he's become Phi Beta Kappa, a two-time All-American mock trial competitor, and a Rhodes scholar.[1] But people don't describe him by his resume details; instead, you'll hear people say, "Neil always has time to talk," "Neil is the most generous person I know," or, most frequently, "Neil probably should control his addiction to coffee."

If you ask Neil about his reputation, he'll tell you two things.

One, Café Pamplona is the best café in Harvard square. Cafe Crema has a nice atmosphere, but doesn't really compare. Dunkin Donuts works if you're in a rush.

And two, he didn't start college focused on others. Instead, a few recent events pushed him to prioritize friends first. Though, he initially feared this would hurt his ambitions, he'd later realize that helping others was critical to his success.

---

1   Alacha, N. (January 18, 2016) Personal Interview

Givers, Matchers, and Takers

In the book Give and Take, Wharton Business School professor Adam Grant examines how helping others drives our success. In particular, he divides people into three categories based on their style of giving. He calls them takers, matchers, and givers. You can already guess who they are. Takers try to extract as much value as possible from others. Matchers try to balance giving and receiving fairly. Givers prefer to help more than they receive.[2]

Let's illustrate these three categories with an example. Imagine you're working on math homework with a group of classmates. The problems are challenging and, as a result, most people are working in small groups. As you survey the room, you notice that people have different approaches to teamwork.

Some individuals seem to be scavenging answers. You know the type. Their eyes are shifty as they look around for the right answer. Once they see a group make progress, they pounce. They walk over and sweetly ask for help. Once they've extracted a solution, they excuse themselves and look around for the next group. Classic taker.

Other individuals seem to do the opposite. Though they might not have all the answers, they're happy to help others catch up. You might see them working with a few of their friends who started late. They sometimes stick with the same group of peers, trying to move ahead as a unit. These are the "Givers."

---

2   Grant, Adam. "Give and take." New York: Viking (2013).

Finally, you notice that some individuals seem to value fairness. Within a study group, they're happy to help others. After all, they themselves received help on other problems. You also notice their reluctance when group outsiders ask for help. You guess: probably a matcher.

In every interaction, we have a choice. Do we try to take as much value as possible, or do we try to help without thought of what we receive in return?

Before you answer, consider another question: which type of person do you think is the most successful? Is it the one who tries to get the most for themselves? The person who gives selflessly? Or maybe the one who values fairness?

To answer that question, Adam Grant and his colleague Dane Barnes began a research project on opticians - a career where professionals face competing interests. On one hand, opticians generate revenue from selling glasses. On the other hand, their job is to serve. Specifically, their goal is to help patients pick the right glasses for their lifestyle.

Grant and Barnes looked at the style of reciprocity for each of the opticians. Some of the opticians were natural givers. They began the conversation by asking you questions about your lifestyle, how you used glasses, and what you were looking for. Their focus was helping you find the right pair even at the cost of not making a sale. Some of the opticians were matchers; they offered discounts and deals to make the trade. Others, finally, were takers. They would flatter shamelessly and say anything to sell their glasses.

So, which of the opticians sold the most? As the researchers found, givers outsold both matchers and takers. Even after controlling for other variables, givers generated thirty percent more revenue than matchers and sixty-eight percent more than takers. Over half of the top sellers were givers.

Perhaps you're skeptical. Sure, givers can do well in a profession where the goal is to help people. But, what if you change the environment? What if we placed them in a more cut-throat world like school?

Why Givers Succeed

In 1998 Belgian researchers began a study of first year medical students. Before their entrance to the school, students were tested on their style of reciprocity. To do this, researchers asked participants if they "enjoy helping others" or "anticipate the needs of others." They then followed the students over the following seven years of medical school.

During the first year, givers did poorly. Students who scored highly on the above questions consistently had a lower GPA than their peers. Then something strange happened. As the students entered their second and third years, the results reversed. Givers began to get better grades than their matcher or taker peers.[3]

What happened? Why did givers do poorly at first and then improve?

---

3   Lievens, Filip, Deniz S Ones, and Stephan Dilchert. "Personality scale validities increase throughout medical school." Journal of Applied Psychology 94.6 (2009): 1514.

Researchers found that the structure of medical school changed over time. As they explained in their published report, "In terms of teaching format, courses in the first year were lecture-based and given to large groups. Evaluations consisted of written exams, testing whether students acquired the necessary knowledge." During the first year, givers gave. They shared their notes, helped others with questions, and sacrificed so that their peers could learn more. As a result, their grades suffered.

After the first year, however, the structure of school changed. The focus moved from knowledge acquisition to working with patients and in smaller groups. Grading shifted from individual test-taking to collaborative patient interactions. Because students and patients preferred working with givers, the givers' GPAs grew on average.

College, and indeed life, follows a similar pattern. Freshman year, we are often subject to large-lectures and zero-sum classes. For the short term, giving might be a losing strategy. But, as time goes on, the benefits of generosity outweigh the cost. Upperclassmen classes are often smaller and have project-based components. The stronger your reputation, the easier it will be to find talented and fun classmates. After you graduate, work becomes even more team-based.[4] Again, giving is the winning strategy.

For college students, there are two main takeaways. First, "giving" is important for the long-term. In the case of medical school, the students who helped others hurt themselves in the

---

4   Heerwagen, Judith, Kevin Kelly, and Kevin Kampschroer. "The Changing Nature of Organisations, Work, and Workplace." Holland (http://www. wbdg. org/design/chngorgwork. php) (2007).

short-term. They spent time helping those around them that they could have spent studying alone. However, as the year went on, the reputation of these students grew. By the end of the first year, other students wanted to work with them. When medical school became more project based, their classmates sought them out as partners.

More self-centered students had the opposite experience. In the short-term, they succeeded by focusing time on their own success. However, as the years went on they lacked vital support from their classmates. Interpersonal relationships gained importance, and as a result, these takers suffered.

The second takeaway is that giving is a better real-life strategy. In college, professors might structure a class to explicitly create a zero-sum environment. If the class grades on a curve, your classmate's "A" reduces your chance of receiving a good grade. In these classes, you might be tempted to act like a taker.

Don't fall into this trap.

Just like in the first year of medical school, there are always situations when taking is marginally better. But, as we explored in the rituals chapter, this is the curse of marginal thinking. In the short-term, you'll gain. But, in the long-term, your reputation will weaken. Even more, you won't be prepared for group work outside college.

But, I'm a College Student... What Can I Give?

Imagine, you've just finished professor Adam Grant's book, Give and Take. You loved it. You're excited about radical giving. And you just drank a bit too much coffee.

You're about to start giving. Right. Now.

You flip open a list of your friends. You scan, looking for a chance to help out.

"What about John?" you think, "He needs help looking for a job!"

So, you begin to wonder, "How can I help John?"

You start thinking. You're trying to remember someone who's had a job. But, you're a sophomore. You don't know anyone who's actually employed.

After five minutes, you begin stroking your early signs of facial hair. Your mind wanders. You start wondering if your mustache and beard will ever connect.

You're stuck. How could you possibly help John out?

"No worries," you think. "Let's look for someone else."

Again, you flip open the list. You scan, looking for someone to help.

"What about Emily? She's looking to do research this semester!"

Again, you rack your head trying to think of a connection. You don't know any professors in need of a helping hand. But, perhaps one of your teaching assistants is!

Excited, you email your section leader for biology. Are they looking for help outside of class?

You eagerly await their reply. One day passes. Then two. Finally, you get a response.

"No."

Oof. Again, you're back to the beginning. A third time, you open the list of friends.

But this time, you're frustrated, dubious even, of the research by Adam Grant. Sure, it's easy for a professor to help out others. They have connections. They have power. They have sage wisdom spewing from their mouth.

What do you have? You're just a student.

You close your list of friends.

You want to be a giver. You also want facial hair. But, you know you'll have to wait.

Many students want to help others, but they fear they have too little to give. Most students don't have powerful connections, life experience, or wealth. Most students don't even have a microwave. A scarcity of resources makes all this advice about giving feel hollow.

Fortunately, there are ways to give that do not require wealth, social capital, or experience. While these may not be immediately apparent, the challenges of life can provide the richest opportunities to help those around us. Coffee lover and mock trial champion Neil Alacha is a distinguished man not because of his intelligence, but because he stood strong for those around him when the time came.

WHEN TRAGEDY STRIKES

Neil Alacha grew up in Brooklyn, New York with a younger sister and high ambitions. In high school, he attended Brooklyn Technical High, joined the debate team, and graduated as valedictorian. He focused relentlessly on succeeding academically.

When Neil first arrived at Harvard, he used the same strategy as he did in high school. He liked economics, and he liked debate. So, he took intermediate economics and joined the mock trial team.

By traditional measures, freshman fall went swimmingly. He did well in class. He impressed upperclassmen on the mock trial team with his fake Brooklyn accent. He even joined Harvard Model Congress – a club known for fun, international travel.

But, though his GPA was high, his Relationship GPA was much lower. In fact, if you asked Neil, he'd say freshman fall didn't feel like a success. He spent the majority of the fall running from class to practice. Though he met people on the team, he didn't feel like he'd committed to anyone in particular. As he put it, "By the end of my fall semester I felt like none of my friendships rivaled those from high school. If I needed to text a friend, I'd still text someone from before college."

When Neil arrived back at school in the spring, he wanted to make a change. His first step was to be vulnerable - to open up a part of himself that he'd been hiding from others.

For years Neil had known that he was gay, but he'd never told his friends and family. So, when he arrived back on campus, he decided to put the third Cinderella Skill into practice and come out about his sexuality. As he recalls, "I just remember sitting in the library, it was like 5:00 AM. I just kept thinking 'you know Neil, the only person who is holding you back is yourself.'" By being vulnerable, Neil grew closer to those around him.

Neil also focused on becoming a better listener, the second Cinderella Skill. During the second semester of his freshman year, he joined the peer-counseling group Room 13, where he learned about non-directive communication. As Neil worked with the group, his ability to listen to others deepened.

Though Neil changed sophomore fall, his fundamental priorities hadn't. Looking for that long coffee chat from the beginning of the chapter? Forget it. Neil had competitions to attend and homework to do.

But, everything changed when tragedy struck Neil's mock trial team.

On February 9, midway through Neil's sophomore spring, the mock trial A team and B team traveled to New York for a regional competition. After two days of fake lawyering, the teams gathered around to hear the results. You could cut the tension with a suspected murder weapon. Finally, after hours of nervous waiting, the tournament announced the results.

The A-team (Neil's team) had won first in the region. But, for the first time in recent memory, the B-team didn't advance to nationals. The news shocked them. In a somber mood, they left the tournament.

As the group contemplated driving back to Boston, Neil proposed an alternative. Why not sleep over at his house in Brooklyn? They could have breakfast and arrive back in Boston by the afternoon. Half the team didn't have morning classes, so Neil led them in one van to his house. The other half took the other van and began the 8-hour drive to Boston.

While Neil directed his van back from the tournament, he made small talk about his favorite coffee from New York. A phone began to ring, and one of the girls in the car answered. Her expression faltered and silence overwhelmed the vehicle.

At around midnight, the other six students had been hit on the New Jersey Turnpike. As they drove along the freeway, a drunk driver had collided with their car, swerving it off the highway. The crash had thrown Angela Mathews, a fellow A-team member, out of the car. She was pronounced dead at the scene.

Two days later, the school held a vigil for Angela in the campus church - Memorial Hall. Tall, imposing, white columns separated pew after pew of students, faculty, and administration.

The mock trial team stood together in the front, holding each other for comfort. They didn't know what was to come. No one did.

Seven students made up the A-team. Every day, they practiced hours together on their case. On weekends with tournaments, they spent 40+ hours working together. As an op-ed in the Crimson, Harvard's daily newspaper, put it , "Harvard Mock Trial is a family bonded by more inside stories, late night practices, humor and brain power than any group of people I know."[5] Now, however, the family had lost one of their own.

For Neil, the first few days back at school were numbing. As he put it, "When I came back, everything felt different. I'd walk back into the dining hall and see people eating and laughing as if nothing had changed. But, it had."

Over the following weeks, Neil spent hundreds of hours with his teammates. He helped them organize sleepovers, dinners, and counseling sessions with the group. Over time, his priorities shifted from himself to those around him.

"I remember earlier that night before the car crash, how distraught we all were about the B team not advancing. At the time it made sense. But, after the car crash, I kept thinking 'how could you be so torn up?' You realize, how silly and insignificant it is."

---

5   "From an Outsider Looking In | Opinion | The Harvard Crimson." 2014. 4 Jun. 2016 <http://www.thecrimson.com/article/2014/9/18/from-an-outsider-looking/>

For Neil, the loss of Angela focused his attention on those around him. Slowly, the traumatic event pushed him to rethink his priorities.

Before the crash, Neil feared that focusing on others would derail his ambitions. He often talked about his dream jobs: Neil wanted to be Secretary of State or a prosecutor for the International Criminal Court. His laser focus on reaching these lofty positions prevented him from going out of his way to give to people.

After the tragedy, Neil started giving more of his time to others - but he didn't become less successful, he became more so. After months of team healing, during which Neil was a tremendous presence, his mock trial teammates took him aside. They wanted him to run for captain of the team.

You might find yourself in the midst of a tragedy, like Neil had. You might merely be struggling to finish your statistics homework with friends late at night. You might be somewhere in between. When things are looking down, give. Reach to bring light into the lives of those around you. While students might not be rich in resources, they have the ability to give in surprising and unique ways. In fact, there are quite a few tangible ways you can start giving now.

THE GIFT OF GRATITUDE

A great way to give is to show appreciation. In a study at Harvard Business School, researchers asked fifty-three students to give feedback on the cover letter of a fictitious student named Eric. In one condition, Eric replied with a short, "I received your feedback on my cover letter." In the other condition, Eric replied, "I received your feedback on my cover letter. Thank you so much! I am really grateful." In the no-gratitude condition, only twenty-five percent of student felt a greater sense of self-worth after helping. In the "thank you" condition, fifty-five percent reported feeling more self-worth. By explicitly thanking someone, you can increase the psychological reward they receive. The gift of gratitude costs you almost nothing and can inspire those around you to give more.[6]

Showing gratitude to others doesn't only help them, it helps yourself long-term. In a follow up study, researchers then asked students in both conditions whether they would help another student with a cover letter. More than double the number of students in the gratitude condition helped compared to the non-gratitude condition. By showing gratitude to others, you make them more likely to help. This isn't too surprising, but it's very easy to forget. After every interaction, make sure you follow up with a quick "thanks."

A great way to use gratitude is to make it part of your routine. Try creating a weekly "day of gratitude." Every week, set aside an hour to write thank-you or birthday cards to those around you. Interestingly, research shows that "chunking" your acts of giving (i.e. doing all of your helping one day a week vs.

---

6   Grant, Adam M, and Francesca Gino. "A little thanks goes a long way: Explaining why gratitude expressions motivate prosocial behavior." Journal of personality and social psychology 98.6 (2010): 946.

over multiple days) improves your underlying happiness more.[7] Happiness, in turn, helps maintain motivation. In the long run, this allows you to give more effectively.

Don't reserve your gratitude for your superiors; show it to nearly everyone in your life. If someone helped you out with homework, send them a quick message saying thank you. At the end of the year, write a thank-you to your professors. Is there a member of staff who works at your dormitory? Make sure they feel appreciated with a quick card. Giving thanks is one of the fastest and cheapest ways to give, so go wild.

CARE PACKAGES

Parents are famous for sending heartwarming care packages throughout college. If you are lucky enough to have received a cardboard box of love, then you know how warm and unique it can make you feel.

Sadly, not everyone receives care packages. You cannot rely on a friend's distant parents to show them love after a rough test, breakup, or cheesecake combustion during a baking competition. You can, however, walk to the store and fill up a bag with their favorite popcorn, trail mix, chocolates, caffeine, movie, pillow, and more. Cap it off with the most ridiculous card you can find or draw.

---

7   Lyubomirsky, Sonja, Kennon M Sheldon, and David Schkade. "Pursuing happiness: the architecture of sustainable change." Review of general psychology 9.2 (2005): 111.

Once you've assembled the package, you can drop it off at their door. For added benefit, assault the door with sticky notes each containing inside jokes and other relevant messages.

Creating a care package can take as little as half an hour. The gift might be the most meaningful thing they received that month. This is such a powerful form of giving that it could almost be considered selfish. According to Scientific America, in reference to a 2006 study in the Proceedings of the National Academy of Sciences, "brains seem to suggest that the joy of being a gift giver may eclipse that of being its recipient."[8] Not only can giving a care package be the perfect pick-me-up for a friend in need, but it can also be the perfect thing to do when you yourself are feeling down.

HELP OTHERS WITH SCHOOL WORK

Thursday night in a Harvard dining hall is a scary, scary place. Many math and science courses have homework due on Friday. As a consequence, dozens of students crowd around tables. Eyes grow bleary and desperation sets in.

Have you ever felt like this? If so, you also know the powerful love you suddenly feel towards a stranger who offers help. One way to give in college is to stick around after you've finished your work. After completing the assignment, you no longer face the same deadline, and you know how best to attack

---

8   "The Psychology Behind Gift-Giving and Generosity - Scientific ..." 2015. 4 Jun. 2016 <http://blogs.scientificamerican.com/literally-psyched/the-psychology-behind-gift-giving-and-generosity/>

the problems. By spending thirty minutes with a group, you could save them dozens of combined hours that night.

Don't stop there. Be proactive with helping. Share your notes. Seek out friends who bombed the last test. Sit next to someone having trouble in lecture. If you're also having trouble, even better. Make sure they know that you're with them through whatever wrath the class might bring.

INTRODUCE FRIENDS

Perhaps you've made new friends after forming alliances against difficult homeworks. While chugging an energy drink at 4:00 AM, you realize that two of your new friends share a passion for hiking - but they've never met each other!

One of the easiest ways to give is to introduce friends. If you notice that two people have a similar interest, then connect them. Send them a quick message saying why you think they should meet. Make sure you show appreciation in the note as well. For example:

Hey Winnie,

Have you met Tigger? He's one of my best friends on campus. He's cheerful, outgoing, and has a stunning vertical jump. He also loves to go on adventures in the forest. I know you were looking for a tree-climbing companion, so I thought I'd put you in touch.

Hey Tigger, I'd like to (electronically) introduce you to Winnie. Winnie (called "Pooh" by friends) is a really close friend of mine. He's thoughtful, caring, and loves honey. He's also a big adventurer - something that I know you like. I know you wanted to spend more time with friends off-campus. So, I thought I'd put you in touch.

Hope you guys get the chance to talk.
-Kanga

BIF YOUR WAY TO A BFF

What is a bif? A bif is trash to you, but treasure to someone else. It's an item that you personally don't want, but one that is too valuable for you to throw away. Examples of bifs might include: plastic swords, walkie-talkies, or anything created in the early 2000s.

We all receive bifs. Imagine, your parents send you a package. You're ecstatic. You never receive mail from your parents. Slowly, you crack open the top.

Your face falls. They're your grandmother's snickerdoodles. By any sane definition, these cookies are delicious - but that unlimited meal plan has laid waste to your waistline and these cookies would deal the finishing blow to your dream of abs.

It's clear you don't want the cookies - but they're too nice to throw away. They're a bif. So, what do you do?

Give them away. Every time you receive something you don't want, don't be disappointed, be ecstatic. They're an opportunity to show that you care about someone else.

A bif is somewhat similar to a regift. Unfortunately, most people think that regifting is a social faux pas. They assume that they'll insult the original giver by regifting. But, research from the London Business School shows that people are happy to have their gifts regifted.[9] Over five studies, researchers looked at both the giver and receiver's perception of gifts. As they found, people who give a gift feel like they've passed on ownership of the item, so the receiver is free to decide what to do with it. Receivers, on the other hand, feel like the original giver still has partial ownership over the gift. Thus, they overestimate how much the giver would care if the item was given to another friend.

Regifting is fine. Your grandma would love for you to share your cookies. Attach a note describing your feelings for a friend. Voila, you've made a friend feel great, and you've vanquished your cinnamon nemesis in the process.

GIVING BECOMES EASIER

When you first begin, giving might not come naturally. You'll have moments where you give coffee to someone who doesn't like caffeine. You'll introduce people who end up hating

---

9   Adams, Gabrielle S, Francis J Flynn, and Michael I Norton. "The Gifts We Keep on Giving Documenting and Destigmatizing the Regifting Taboo." Psychological science 23.10 (2012): 1145-1150.

each other. You'll probably thank a friend for something they didn't do. Giving can be hard.

Give more, and giving will become easier. Through practice, you become more aware of what others need. If your roommate likes having someone to talk to at night, be that person. If they have a big test, write a small note rooting for them. Adapt to their reactions. As you give more, you'll no longer have to ask "How can I help?" Instead, you'll already know.

Your network will also grow more supportive over time. When you give to someone else, you establish a norm which makes it more likely that they'll pass on the kindness. Helping is a virtuous cycle. The more you give, the more your friends want to give. This can culminate in an incredibly loving, and therefore powerful, group of people.

For Neil Alacha, after the car accident he realized that he could help most by offering his time and love to his teammates. He gave, and, as a side effect of that, his friends wanted him to succeed.

Becoming Coffee Shop Neil

After the accident, Neil's commitment to others began permeating everything he did. At the same time, opportunities started coming to him.

First, Neil ran for captain of the Mock Trial team - he won. For the next year, he focused intensely on developing his younger teammates. And, overtime, his commitment to others paid off.

In April 2015, a little more than a year after Angela's death, the Harvard Mock Trial team won the national championship.

During Neil's junior spring, members of Harvard Model Congress urged Neil to run for president. His honest and caring nature had earned the club's respect, and they wished to be led by such a person. Again, his focus on helping others had led him to another leadership role.

In the long run, Neil didn't sacrifice his academic dreams - he made them possible by investing in those around him. Eventually, he would go on to be selected as one of twenty-four juniors for Phi Beta Kappa, an award for the best academic students in the college. About a year later, the Rhodes Trust would choose Neil to become a Rhodes scholar - in part because of his leadership in mock trial and model congress.

It is unlikely Neil would have become the leader he did without having first become a giver. Success is often granted by those around us. By proactively helping, giving, and caring for others, you unintentionally build a community of people who conspire to make you successful. Being smart is not enough - give often.

PART II

Your Relationship GPA

PRIORITIZATION

PROFESSORS & MENTORS

DATING

FAMILY & OLD FRIENDS

8
PRIORITIZATION

"Action expresses priorities."

- Mahatma Gandhi

Thirty minutes into the dinner, Ben's phone lit up. As he glanced at it, he could barely make out the fluorescent text.[1]

"Ben, where are you? The show starts in 30 minutes! - Jason"

Ben clicked off his phone and looked up. He was surrounded by friends: fifteen men sitting around a long wooden table. Two guys to Ben's right were joking about failed love interests. A fellow senior reached over Ben to grab a slice of cheesecake. A friend in the corner stared with respect at another gulping wine.

"What a strange combination of debauchery and home," Ben thought to himself. Then as he looked down, he saw his phone flash again.

---

1   Blumstein, B. (January 17, 2016) Personal Interview

"Ben, where are you? This could be amazing for your music. - Jason"

Quietly, Ben got out of his chair. He pushed it smoothly back into the table. A few of his friends offered hugs and wishes of good luck as he left. With a final glance over his shoulder, Ben stepped out of the house into the cool streets of Cambridge.

Before walking to his room, Ben looked back briefly at the dinner party; their shadows danced against a diaphanous window screen. "What a group..." he thought wistfully to himself. Then he turned and his mind shifted back to Chance.

He looked down at his phone. "Don't worry, I'm coming!" he replied. "I wouldn't miss meeting Chance the Rapper for the world."

As Ben walked back to his room to change, he thought about the opportunity that life just presented. It could change the direction of his music career.

The *Bare Essentials*

For the past five years, Ben Blumstein had trained to be a professional musician. Born in Seattle, Washington, his dad gave him his first microphone at fourteen for Christmas. The simple gift was enough to get him hooked.

Throughout high school, Ben wrote beats for himself and his friends. Then when he entered Harvard College, he began to rap.

From the beginning, it was clear Ben had a sheer talent for writing. His first album, *Bare Essentials*, featured the lines "Loki, the gates are open / Fade to black, wandering Odin gone ravin' [raven] mad."[2] In doing so, he might have been the first person ever to reference two Norse gods in one chorus. The man was a hip hop Dr. Seuss.

Ben also had an incredible ability to make others feel comfortable and cared for. In his junior year, he joined the counseling group Room 13, mentioned in Chapter Four. Overtime, he developed a group of friends who were loving, caring, and viciously loyal.

When Ben began his music career at Harvard, his friend group was the first to support him. His friends, especially those in his grade, insisted that Ben perform his first concert on campus. Ben's first album used "nature rap" - a form of rap that weaves tribal instrumentals with hip hop. So, his friends wore face paint, costumes, and insisted on carrying Ben out to the stage. "I was singing a ridiculous nature rap to a basement of sixty sweaty college students. But, to me, it felt like TD Garden… the kind of love in the room was unquestioning. Everyone just completely bought in."

The summer before senior year, Ben lived in L.A. with his good friend Jason. During this time, Ben worked on his music and reached out to fellow artists. One of the musicians Ben looked up to most was "Chance the Rapper." For those who don't know who Chance is, he "did a ton of drugs and did better than

---

2   Bared Grillz. Bare Essentials (2013)

all (his) alma mater," according to a line from his second album. He has been featured on Kanye West's Life of Pablo album, rapped on Macklemore's second album, and has been remixed by Skrillex. Ben's admiration for Chance motivated him to exercise the first Cinderella Skill and reach out to Chance's producer. After a quick chat, the producer promised Ben that he'd get in touch if Chance ever played in Cambridge.

A few weeks before Ben's graduation, and almost a year later, he received an email from the producer. Chance would be playing in the Sinclair - a club a few hundred feet from Harvard Yard. The producer wanted Ben to meet Chance, so he put him and Jason on the "guest list." He would gain backstage access and spend the night with the performers.

For Ben, Chance's show represented a once in a lifetime opportunity. Not only was Chance someone Ben looked up to, but the rapper had access. In a cutthroat world of music, knowing a few of the right people could mean the difference between making it and not.

But, the show came on an unfortunate date. His friends had decided to throw a dinner for graduating seniors. That dinner, the one that Ben was attending, was one of Ben's final opportunities to see his graduating friends. Coincidentally, Chance's show landed perfectly on the dinner's date.

As Ben walked back to his room to change his clothes, he began to feel a strange mix of emotions: excitement to meet Chance, but, alongside it, a sinking sense of guilt. Should he have left the dinner? Was he doing the right thing?

The story of Ben illustrates a painful truth: we face trade-offs with relationships. We'd like to be friends with everyone, but we can't. We have limits to our time, our energy, and even our mental space. We have to make choices: what do we prioritize first? When rapper meets dinner party, which do we choose?

To understand the importance of prioritization, we'll explore the Christmas card habits of Brits, how gaining weight can be contagious, and why Southwest Airlines is so great while being so bad at service.

WHY YOU DON'T RECEIVE 500 CHRISTMAS CARDS

Roughly twenty years ago, evolutionary psychologist Charles Dunbar began a study of Christmas card giving in Britain. At that time, it was hard to measure the number of people in a social group. To get around this, Dunbar used Christmas cards as a proxy for a relationship. As he explained, "In Western societies…the exchange of Christmas cards represents the one time of year when individuals make an effort to contact all those individuals within their social network whose relationships they value."[3] Therefore, by knowing how many Christmas cards people sent, you could estimate how many relationships they maintained.

After the researchers tallied the number of cards sent, they found that each person received cards from roughly 150

---

3   Hill, Russell A, and Robin IM Dunbar. "Social network size in humans." Human nature 14.1 (2003): 53-72.

individuals (counting each member in a household). The number 150, didn't surprise Dunbar. In fact, it supported his hypothesis: humans have a limited social network size. The largest number for a social network is around 150 or less.

Dunbar initially discovered the number because of his work with primates. He hypothesized that primates had bigger brains than most species because they need to maintain a high number of social connections. The larger the brain size of primates, the larger their social network. When Dunbar compared humans to other primates, he found that we fit along the same line. Our maximum community size was roughly 150.

As Dunbar looked throughout history, he saw 150 pop up repeatedly. 150 was the size of a Roman company. Most Hutterite communes - Amish-like communities - in the U.S. split off after reaching 100 to 200 people in size. The world's remaining hunter-gathering tribes top off at 150.[4] Just as humans have physical limitations, we have social limitations too.

Dunbar visualized our relationships as a set of concentric circles. The outermost layer of 150 - or "Dunbar's number" - is composed of causal relationships. You can think of these people as the ones you would invite to your wedding. The next level is your fifty closest relationships. These are the people you see often. You might invite them to a dinner party, but you wouldn't necessarily call your relationships "intimate." Next, we have your top fifteen. These are the people you turn to for emotional

---

4   "The Limits of Friendship - The New Yorker." 2014. 4 Jun. 2016 <http://www.newyorker.com/science/maria-konnikova/social-media-affect-math-dunbar-number-friendships>

comfort and support. Finally, there are your most important five. These include family members and closest friends.

Dunbar's research shows that we have limits to our friendships. In college, we'd like to maintain all of our relationships. But, we can't. Instead, we have to make trade-offs: do we go to a party with new friends? Or do we hang out in our room with our roommate? Do we call our family? Or do we talk to our high school best friend? Prioritization is necessary because we can't maintain relationships with everyone.

Some people say we are the average of the five people we spend the most time with, and at the core of this simple adage is truth. The people around us shape the people we become. As research shows, our social network influences our happiness, our grades, and even, surprisingly, whether we gain the freshman 15.

Avoiding The Freshman 15? Avoid Your Roommate.

In 2007, a pair of social scientists named Nicholas Christakis and James Fowler wanted to understand the effect of relationships on health. They began by looking for a longitudinal study that followed health and social connections. After months of searching, they stumbled upon the Framingham Heart Study.

The Framingham study followed the lives of 15,000 individuals in Framingham, Massachusetts. The study began in 1948 and has continued to this day. The original researchers wanted to understand the relationship between cholesterol and heart health. To do so, they tracked the health of individuals for the next sixty years. In each check-up, they asked participants to list the people they knew around Framingham. Christakis and Fowle used that data to construct a social map of the town. They'd hit upon a social scientist's goldmine.

After two years, the team had before them a map with 5124 subjects and 53,228 connections. The team created an animated diagram of the nodes on a computer to visualize the body weight data of each of participant from 1971 t0 2003. Each person appeared on the map as a dot whose size was proportional to the weight of the individual. When the researchers animated the map over the years, they noticed a pattern. People didn't gain weight randomly. Instead, they gained weight with those around them.[5]

The researchers were intrigued by the results: was weight gain… contagious? Out of curiosity, they repeated the experiment with smoking habits. Again, the effect was the same. People smoked if their close relationships smoked. But, if a few of their friends began to quit, they'd be likely to quit with them. Groups started and stopped smoking together.

In fact, the effect wasn't just contained to direct relationships. As the researchers found, participants were twenty percent more likely to become obese if the friend of a friend did. This correlation remained true even if the intermediate contact gained no weight at all. Repeatedly, the study found that we affect

5   Fowler, James H, and Nicholas A Christakis. "Estimating peer effects on health in social networks: a response to Cohen-Cole and Fletcher; Trogdon, Nonnemaker, Pais." Journal of health economics 27.5 (2008): 1400.

(and are affected by) people up to three degrees of separation away. If your friend's roommate's boyfriend has a great day, you just might too.

Underlying their research is a simple theme: our peers influence who we become. If your best friend gains weight, you are three times more likely to gain weight yourself. Similarly, for every happy friend you have, your personal happiness increases by nine percent. Choosing who we spend time with isn't just a social question; it's a matter of health, happiness, and success.

Luckily, the business world has researched prioritization for the past few decades: they call it strategy. When companies have limited resources, how do they allocate them to do the most good? When we have limited time, how do we share it to create the most meaningful relationships?

In strategy 101, MBA's learn about famed economist Michael Porter's theories. His research focuses on business; but, we can apply its lessons to our social lives in college. In his framework, there are two ways firms succeed: operational efficiency and strategic success.[6]

Operational efficiency describes making the most of the resources you have. For a company, this could mean decreasing costs or increasing production rate. If your business produced cars, improving operational efficiency would mean growing the number of cars you create each day. As Michael Porter put it, " (Operational Efficiency) refers to any number of practices

---

6   Porter, Michael E. Competitive strategy: Techniques for analyzing industries and competitors. Simon and Schuster, 2008.

that allow a company to better utilize its inputs by, for example, reducing defects in products or developing better products faster."[7] These improvements on the margin prove vital when they add up.

Strategic success, on the other hand, is positioning yourself to succeed. These are the high-level decisions for companies. If you're an automotive manufacturer, do you start investing in electric cars or self-driving cars? Or none of the above? Without the right strategy, it doesn't matter how hard you work - you'll be moving in the wrong direction.

Up till now, we've described the "Cinderella Skills" as ways to connect more effectively with others. In many respects, these skills improve the "operational efficiency" of relationships. The faster you can connect with someone, the better the current relationships will be. But, as Porter argues, operational efficiency isn't enough for success. To be truly successful, you need to focus on strategy.

WHY YOU HAVE TO MAKE HARD CHOICES

You might not think it, but Southwest Airlines is something of a rebel in the aviation world. The company doesn't use assigned seating. They only have one type of plane - the 737. And, have you ever flown business class on Southwest? No? Well, no one has. The airline only has one type of seat: coach.[8]

---

7   Porter, Michael E. On competition. Harvard Business Press, 2008.
8   Porter, Michael E. "What is strategy." Strategy for business: A reader 625 (2002).

Traditional airlines - not Southwest - try to do it all. They stop at big airports. They travel long distances. They distinguish between different types of passengers: first, business, and economy. In doing so, they try to attract everyone from first-time flyers to business travelers.

Southwest could care less about pleasing everyone. Instead, their focus is providing low-cost, convenient service to customers. That means they've made difficult choices. Southwest flights do not provide in-flight meal services. The airline does not provide inline bagging. Compared to other airlines, Southwest hires fewer gate agents. Instead, they've introduced electronic check-ins. For passengers, this is less convenient. But, for the airline, the reduced staff helps lower costs. The low prices in turn attract a loyal customer base and has helped the airline grow into the largest domestic carrier in the United States.

In 1993, Continental Airlines tried to mimic Southwest's success. They began by establishing a subsidiary airline named "Continental Lite" in an attempt to copy Southwest's cost-cutting tactics. Continental Lite planes removed their first class seats, eliminated meals, and lowered fares. But, Continental's management wouldn't agree to all of Southwest's radical changes. Part of why Continental had been successful in the past was excellent service. Continental Lite couldn't help but continue to employ travel agents, different types of planes, and baggage checking.

Continental refused to make certain trade-offs; part of their company still used the traditional airline model while

"Continental Lite" did not. Unlike Southwest, this led to the worst of both worlds. Continental Lite delivered on its promise, cheap flights with few amenities. But, the company lost money as a result.

Two years after Continental Lite began, the company declared it would shut down the subsidiary. In the previous two years, they had lost a $140 million. Since then, twenty-six vice-presidents had left the company.

The case of Continental illustrates a fundamental principle: you can't do it all. No matter how hard you work on developing your "Cinderella Skills," without prioritization, you'll spend time with the wrong people.

A Moment Of Realizing Priorities

As Ben opened his room door, he took a deep, calming breath. The idea of meeting Chance was feeling more and more like a reality. He walked to his closet and picked out his favorite shirt. As he looked at himself in the mirror, the words of one friend kept reverberating in his head.

"This is a once-in-a-lifetime opportunity for you. You need to do it."

The walk to the Sinclair, the concert venue, goes directly through Harvard's main campus. As Ben marched onwards, he passed physical reminders of the past four years: his room sophomore and junior year, the street he and his friends would stumble down after a late night, and even the location of the dinner party.

When Ben arrived at the Sinclair, he immediately approached the bouncer. The burly man waved him in impatiently; he was on the list. But, for some reason, Ben hesitated. He began to think back to his first show with his friends - the moment when he entered the makeshift stage in front of a crowd of poorly dressed, but wildly enthusiastic friends. Ben remembered how his girlfriend had talked to him after the show. Sometimes, she didn't agree with the friends Ben had chosen. But, during the concert, she saw the incredible loyalty and love that his friends felt for each other.

Suddenly, Ben knew he'd made the wrong choice. "I was like 'What the hell am I doing...' I can't believe I'm passing up my final time with my friends for maybe a good networking opportunity. It was a moment of realizing priorities."

In front of the bouncer, Ben turned a complete 360. He walked a few blocks to where the dinner party was being held and then paused in front of the door, wondering if he made the right choice. Shaking his head in determination, he stepped inside. The table of seniors turned to look at him, confused.

Ben addressed the group, "Guys, I messed up.... I almost turned into what I don't want, which is ungrateful of people who are there for you, people who are totally devoted to you. You guys."

As Ben learned, prioritization in the abstract is easy. Of course you should spend time with the people you care about most. Everyone knows that. When pressed, most people can say which relationships they value highest.

The tricky part is aligning our priorities with our actions. We might say that we prioritize our family. Yet in reality, we find ourselves spending ten times more time talking to our roommates. We might convincingly rank friends higher than love-interests. But, we spend every weekend with our new boyfriend and his chiseled abs.

Prioritization is the invisible framework underpinning all relationships. To be frank, it isn't easy. To prioritize, you need to make uncomfortable choices.

With that said, we push you to make these difficult decisions. Knowing who you prioritize allows you to focus on what matters most. It will reduce guilt when choosing between opportunities. It will make calling home easier. It might even help you become a better friend.

Define Your Values

Imagine, you're talking with your roommate late at night. His body lazes over the top of your bunk bed. Your body lazes over the bottom. He's snacking on cheesecake. You wish you had cheesecake.

You've started reading a book on "prioritizing relationships." You hadn't thought much about ranking your relationships, after all, who has? Maybe your roommate. He always seems confident. Plus, he has an endless supply of lactose-based sweets. If that doesn't scream prioritization, nothing does. He must know how his relationships compare. You ask him.

In fact, he does. When you ask, he barely pauses before giving you the list.

"First is family," he says, "Obviously."

"Next, I'd probably say roommates." he continues.

"Then, meeting new people."

"Then current friends."

"Eh, then perhaps romantic relationships last."

Over the next few weeks, you watch your roommate. Maybe, if you observe his prioritization, you'll be able to do it yourself. You just learned about osmosis in biology 101. You didn't read the chapter, but, you assume this is how it works.

Over time, however, you grow confused. You haven't seen your roommate talk to his parents once. He spends most of his time at parties drinking with friends. And, when he's back in the room? Well, let's just say, you're acutely aware of what's happening on the top bunk.

His actions don't match his priorities.

As you talk to more friends, you realize this is almost universally true. One friend ranked their significant other highly, but spends more time with their Xbox than with their steady. Your professor says that students are her "number one priority," but she replies to your emails once a week at best. Even you fall into this trap. You'd say your high school friends are the most important people in your life, but you only speak to them once every one month or two.

Is everyone a hypocrite?

Yes and no. As an experiment, ask a friend to rank their relationships. They probably won't have an immediate answer. Give them time and push them to finish. After a while, they'll write down a list. After they've completed the list, ask them to look at their calendar this week. Does the time they spend roughly match their supposed rankings?

In general, we face two problems when prioritizing relationships. First, few people are explicit about preferences. That is, few people have even thought about their relationship strategy. Second, people's actions don't align with their stated preferences. This incongruency could either mean that they need to change their behavior (e.g. spend more time with high school friends), or they need to reorder their priorities (e.g. place high school friends under college friends).

In economics, this is the difference between "stated preferences" and "revealed preferences." Stated preferences are what people believe they desire. For example, you might think you'd pay $100 for your roommate not to invite "guests" into the top bunk. But, if actually given the option, you might only pay $50 - you're broke. $100 is your "stated preference" and $50 is your "revealed preference."

The first step for prioritization is aligning your stated preferences with your revealed preferences. Doing this requires deep introspection and uncomfortable decisions. To help, we'll show you a system developed over the past five years by some of the people who do it best. We call the technique "Relationship Factoring."

RELATIONSHIP FACTORING

CFAR, the Center For Applied Rationality, helps ambitious people make better decisions. Created in 2012 by an ex-NASA researcher, a statistician, and two mathematics PhDs, CFAR charges eager participants thousands of dollars to help them overcome common cognitive mistakes. If you want to become a better planner, predictor, or goal-setter, you ought to talk to CFAR.[9]

One CFAR workshop is Goal Factoring. The program asks you to consider all the ways you spend your time on a regular basis. Perhaps a few hours studying, a coffee every morning at Starbucks, pizza and drinks on Fridays, an hour of social media, and so on. After you have detailed when and how you spend your time, the workshop starts drilling down by asking why. Why do you get a coffee at Starbucks in the mornings? Because you hope to meet someone new in a coffee shop. Why? Because you can't work up the courage to ask the barista's name. Why?

---

9   "Inside The Rationality Movement That Has Silicon Valley Buzzing With ..." 2014. 5 Jun. 2016 <http://www.fastcompany.com/3037333/most-creative-people/inside-the-rationality-movement-that-has-silicon-valley-buzzing-with-po>

Because you are nervous about the way people perceive you. And so on.

Like factoring large numbers in math, goal factoring breaks down your routines and habits. Eventually, you get to the root motivations behind your actions. You are a broke college student buying overpriced coffee. You have a crush and feel insecure. Is drinking a calorie heavy pumpkin spice triple pump latte chino every morning going to improve this situation? Or can you change your actions to better address your motivations?

Goal factoring is an excellent way to get at your core desires. So, we've repurposed it around relationships. We'll show you "Relationship Factoring" to help you discern which of your relationships matter most.

Part 1: Defining Your Values (The Boat Game)

Is being a good roommate more important than being a good friend? At this point in your life, would you rather have a significant other or a significant mentor? If you call home, do you call your family or your high school friends? Defining your values is difficult. To help you do it, we'll explain a game that's been used for generations of camping trip leaders at Harvard: The Boat Game.

Step 1: Write Down Seven Types Of Relationships

By types, we mean a general category of people. For example, this could include "friends," "family," "best friends," or "mentors." For Stephen, his seven were (in no particular order) friends, special people, family, roommates, mentors, new people, and the Franklin Fellowship - his favorite student group. For Greg, his seven were hang-out friends, best friends, acquaintances, family, mentors, significant other, and computer science friends. To make categories more concrete, write one or two examples of each grouping. The groups won't be perfect, but it will give you a rough outline of your current relationships. Finally, transfer the seven relationships onto seven small pieces of paper. Keep the seven pieces of paper with you.

Step 2: Begin The Story

For this next section, you'll have to tell yourself a story. If you play this game in a group, one person should become the storyteller. We'll give you an example story but feel free to adapt it as you like.

Story: Your Island Cruise Adventure

Ahh…. what a beautiful day in the Bahamas. You're wearing a swimsuit, sunglasses, and a thick layer of SPF 100. You can't wait for this cruise to start.

Finally, the ship's horn blows. On cue, you begin walking to the ship's kitchen area. Rumor says there is an unlimited supply of cheesecake in the buffet. You plan to find that rumor. Then you plan to eat it.

After thirty minutes of searching, you're no closer to your creamy destination. You have stumbled upon shuffleboard – which, as you realize, might be the most boring activity on earth. It's too late, however, because a seventy-four-year-old woman challenges you to a game. In frustration, you slam a shuffleboard disc against the wall of the ship.

You're hungry. You're tired. And now Martha is beating you at a tropical version of curling.

Cruises suck.

Suddenly, you hear a voice over the loudspeaker.

"Attention! Attention! We have an emergency. A shuffleboard disc has punctured our lower deck wall. We're gaining water fast."

You slowly step back from the shuffleboard court, your finger pointing at Martha.

"In order to prevent sinking, we need to lose weight. We ask each passenger to throw overboard two of the seven pieces of luggage they brought."

Step 3: Lose Two Items

Look back over your seven relationships. Select two pieces of paper and crumple them up before placing them in a pile in front of you.

Story: Your Island Cruise Adventure (Continued)

"How inconsiderate!" you say to the passenger next to you, "Who would possibly puncture the wall of a cruise ship?"

You shrug your shoulders, ignorant of the forming crowd.

"Okay, no more joking around. I will find this cheesecake."

Your search resumes. This time, as you wander around the lower deck, you pass by the board game room. You see Martha, your shuffleboard nemesis, playing bridge.

She waves. You glare.

You turn into a bathroom. "How does a sewage system on a cruise ship even work?" you wonder. In any case, you plan to find out.

Five minutes later, you flush. "Well, that wasn't too bad," you reflect.

Suddenly, along with a distant Wilhelm scream, you hear a scratchy noise over the loudspeaker.

"Attention! Attention! We have an emergency. Our sanitary system appears to have just malfunctioned. A containment unit exploded, puncturing the hull. We're gaining water fast."

You glance down at the toilet. You notice a small sign above it "PLEASE NO TOILET PAPER."

"Was that always there?" you wonder.

"In order to prevent sinking, we need to lose weight. We ask each passenger to throw overboard two of the seven pieces of luggage they brought."

Step 4: Lose Two More Items

Look back over your five remaining relationships. Choose the three that are most important to you. Then, discard the other two in a separate pile.

Story: Your Island Cruise Adventure (Continued)

"Jeez this cheesecake is hard to find... perhaps a ship member would know!"

Somehow the thought invigorates you. Feeling significantly lighter, you walk out of the bathroom.

Immediately, you spot a crew member in the hall. He's wearing a sailor hat and a full blue suit. He obviously loves cheesecake.

"Oy!" you yell. He turns. "Where can I find the dessert section?"

He looks at you quizzically, as if recognizing you from WANTED posters around the ship. Finally, he shrugs his shoulders. Then he points up.

"Up?" you wonder. But, after all, he is wearing a blue suit. He must know the way.

As you walk to where he had pointed, you spot a small service hatch above him. You look both ways, but the man in blue is already gone. So, you jump, grab the dangling lever, and pull-down.

As you start shimmying up the ladder, you hear a gruff sound come over the speaker

"Attention! Attention! We have an emergency. We've detected a security breach on the port side. Please stay calm. We have sent a crew to investigate."

"Man, what a dangerous cruise." you think, "I wonder if all ships are like this?"

You continue climbing. The intercom continues blaring.

"Unfortunately, we've redirected crew from the water pumping station. We're going to ask each passenger to throw over one more piece of luggage."

Step 5: Lose One More Item

Look at your remaining three relationships. Now choose the two most important. Discard the third in a separate pile.

Story: Your Island Cruise Adventure (Continued)

As you climb the final rung, you bump up against a small hatch. You open it and pop your head out. You're in the central kitchen. And there's cheesecake. Everywhere.

Crew members scurry around, frantically carrying what appears to be a large water hose. "Maybe it's for the frosting?" you wonder. In any case, it doesn't matter. You're finally here.

You see a piece of cheesecake lying on a table, feet from the escape hatch. You scramble to your feet and walk over to it.

You're standing over the most glorious beige dessert you've ever seen. It's as if your mother also spread SPF 100 on it. Delicious. Now, the only thing you need is a fork.

You see a small drawer labeled "cutlery" to your right. Excited, you pull it out.

Unfortunately, you used a bit too much force. A single fork pops out of the drawer and falls down the open hatch. Suddenly...

"Attention! Attention! We have an emergency. Crew members have reported a fork-shaped puncture hole at the bottom of the hull. We are currently investigating. "

Undeterred, you turn to the cheesecake. Mouth watering, you scoop up the piece with your bare hands and take a bite of your hard earned treasure.

"The reports have been confirmed. We're going to ask each passenger to throw over a final piece of luggage."

Step 6: Lose One More Item

Look at your remaining two relationships. Now choose the most important. Place the other relationship in a pile next to you.

Step 7: List Backwards

Take out another sheet of paper and use it to rank the relationships from one to seven. One is the relationship that you kept with you until the end. Six and seven are the relationships you threw out first.

Step 8: Review Your Priorities

Look back over your relationships. They should be ranked in order of importance. If you want to switch one or two, do so; the goal is to give you a general idea of your priorities.

Let's go over the steps briefly:

Step 1: Write Down Your Relationships

Step 2: Begin The Story

Step 3: Lose Two Items

Step 4: Lose Two More Items

Step 5: Lose One More Item

Step 6: Lose One More Item

Step 7: List Backwards

Step 8: Review Your Priorities

Your Relationship GPA

The Boat Game: Why We Do It

It's difficult to say how important something is unless you compare it to something else. For example, if we asked, "How important are your friends to you?" You'd probably answer, "Crucial!" If we then asked, "How important is your family?" You might say once again, "Crucial." You undoubtedly believe both. Friends are important. Family is also important. But, how do you know which is more important? You have to compare.

We use the boat game to create lists of priorities because telling a story is fun, and because writing out "your top seven relationships" is a surprisingly complex task - there are 5040 unique orderings. By incrementally losing two relationships, and then one, you can make the task achievable.

The final product of the boat game is a ranking of relationships. Granted, each person's rankings mean different things. For some people, their number one will be 500% more significant than their number two. For others, number one and two will feel almost interchangeable.

This ranking is helpful, but it needs to be developed further before it can offer actionable information. As we saw with your roommate, people don't always follow what they say. When that happens, you need to notice the discrepancy. Is it because you're spending time incorrectly? Or because you're deceiving yourself about who really matters? What happens when your words and your actions contradict?

Part Two: Notice Inconsistencies

You've done it. You finally finished "the boat game". You cried after throwing your "siblings" overboard. You smiled after throwing your "roommates" to the sharks. You even ate some cheesecake. You're feeling 100% confident about your priorities.

Returning to normal life feels easy. You go to class, you study, you even attend a few parties.

Okay, one party. But still.

Everything feels normal until Friday night rolls around. Friday night, for your roommate, is Call Of Halo Night. It's a night of non-stop video games - your favorite kind of games.

You have breakfast plans with a friend the next morning, so you want to go to bed early. But, as you walk into the common room your roommate spots you. "Hey! Would you like to play a round?"

"Uh, sure," you reply. After all, what's the problem with fifteen minutes?

Three hours later, you stand up, waving off cries to play "one more round." You hadn't planned to decapitate 180 zombies that night, but you did. You fall asleep immediately when your body hits the bed.

As you arrive late to breakfast the next morning, you feel a small pang of guilt. Why did you spend so much time with your roommate last night? Hadn't you ranked him last in the boat game?

The more you review your past week, the more guilty you feel. You ranked high school friends first. Yet, you didn't call them once. You ranked best friends second, yet you spent the entire weekend with acquaintances and the undead. And family? You might have sent them a text. You can't remember.

The Hour Game

In the boat game, you prioritized. Now, let's find out - does your time match those rankings? For this exercise, go back to the last week you were in school. (For those not in college, use your most recent busy week.) Now, tally up the number of hours you spent on each category of relationships.

A couple of tips:

- *Write down examples of people in each category. Make explicit who falls into which group.*

- *Look at a calendar to get an accurate look at your time. If you don't use a calendar, go back to messages or emails you sent between people.*

- *Use your last week in school, not a "general week". We've found using a "general week" leads to an idealized number of hours spent. We want the true figures.*

Once finished, look for inconsistencies. Perhaps you ranked family first, but you spent only twenty minutes talking to them last week. One participant who completed this exercise noticed that she highly valued her high school friends. When she looked at an average week, she didn't spend a minute on them.

If you find an inconsistency, don't worry. Most people will. But, it's important to ask, why does your inconsistency exist?

Perhaps you need to re-rank your priorities. For example, we've found that many students rank family near the top of their list, and yet when they are pressed about time allocation, they report ten to twenty minutes per a week on family members. Perhaps, at this time in their life, they should prioritize their peers first.

On the other hand, you could be confident about your values, but how you spend your time doesn't show it. In this case, you might need to redistribute your time. If you value roommates highly, and yet you spend little time in your room, plan to study there over the next few weeks. If you value family highly, but you find yourself never calling home, perhaps make a weekly ritual to call a sibling.

It is worth noting that time is only one measurement you could compare against priority. You could also compare gifts given, conversations had, or meals eaten. Not all time is equal - an hour with your significant other could be dramatically more meaningful than five with your classmates working on a project. That being said, time is a good place to start when considering how your actions compare with your feelings. While there is no right or wrong way to allocate your time, we do believe is that there is power in knowing what you value. Once you do, you can focus on the right people however you see fit.

PART 3: RECALIBRATE

After the zombie-apocalypse debacle, you're determined. You know that you value your best friends highly and you want to increase how much time you spend with them. You've decided to do what any rational person would - you're going to start running.

For most people this might not seem like the logical action for other goals. Losing five pounds? Sure, go running. Doing a marathon next year? Fine. Start running. But, "Spend time with your best friends?" Running might not seem like the logical choice.

You know your friends well, however. One of them, Pat, has asked you to go on runs throughout the school year. You've always refused. You had homework. You had a test coming up. You'd already run that day (now you're lying too).

But, what if "running" wasn't the point? What if Pat just wanted to hang out? Running just happened to be a mechanism to do so.

You send Pat a message, "Hey, I'd love to start running - do you want to be running buddies this semester?"

The reply was almost too fast - as if she'd been waiting.

"Yes! I'd love to!"

Then comes the much harder message: "Wanna go for a jog tomorrow at... 8:00 AM?"

You throw your phone on your bed. What have you just done?

As you see the phone light up with a response, you begin to feel a bit better. You might not like running. But, you do like Pat. At least you'll definitely hang out now.

Institutionalize A Commitment

What inconsistencies do you have? Whatever they may be, consider why they occur. In most cases, the cause is a lack of intentionality. Think back to the first day of class. Remember looking around the classroom for an open seat. At the time, you probably weren't thinking much about the importance of that seat. After all, you could move at the start of the next class if you really wanted.

Now, think back to the third week of class. Remember walking in and sitting down. You probably didn't think much about where to sit. In fact, you probably sat in the same place you did the day before. Most likely, you'll sit there again tomorrow.

Imagine you met some of the students outside of class and enjoyed talking. In particular, you had a great conversation with a guy named Sean about the difference between Swiss Army knives and Swiss cheese. When you go back to class the next day, you realize that Sean sits in a different table than you. What do you do? Do you abandon your traditional seat to see Sean? Or do you continue sitting where you are?

Notice how difficult this change is. Even a few weeks into a semester, we've established a habit. In a class with no assigned seating, we feel an obligation to stay in the same pattern. Our routine outside of classrooms is similar. No one tells us what to do, but over time, we develop patterns of living. As time goes on, changing these habits becomes challenging.

The key is nudging your behavior in a new direction. In the case of "spending more time with best friends," you can't completely reorder your life. You wouldn't change your classes to hang out with friends, nor would your friends want you to. Instead, you asked if a friend could go on a morning run - an easy addition to the schedule.

For this final section, look back at your inconsistencies. You'll probably be able to judge which ones are most important (to you). When you do, think about small rituals you could add with them. Again, we want you to focus on rituals instead of one-off activities because these are long-term problems. If you spend more time with your friends this week, but not the rest of the semester, you haven't changed.

We understand, prioritization is hard. At times, you'll feel uncomfortable neglecting someone. Other times you'll miss out on new opportunities.

The alternative, however, is worse. At the end of four years, you don't want to look back and think "I spent college with the wrong people." Instead, you'll want to have invested in the people that matter. If you don't sacrifice for who you love, you might find out who you love will be the sacrifice.

In the case of Harvard student and rapper Ben Blumstein, we'd like to say he got everything he wanted that night. He didn't. Ben didn't meet Chance. Ben didn't show Chance his album. Ben didn't even talk to the producer. His friend Jason, who went to the concert, did however. By 3:00 AM, Jason had hung out with Chance for hours, even taking photos with him at the after party.

Ben gave up one opportunity of a lifetime for another - being with his friends for a final time. And though, we can make predictions about what would have happened to Ben had he gone to the concert, we should also step back and look at what has happened to Ben since he didn't. As a senior, Ben had become one of the most respected and well-loved students at Harvard. His reputation came from small acts like these - loyal choices that few people would make, but that most people wish they would.

Ben's success didn't just come from making hard decisions; it also came from a series of critical relationships. Mentors, in particular, helped guide Ben through his most ambiguous choices. As we'll explore, mentors can be the difference between feeling challenged and feeling stressed, trying out new things and sticking to what you know, or gazing up at the stars and truly reaching them.

PRIORITIZATION

PROFESSORS & MENTORS

DATING

FAMILY & OLD FRIENDS

9

PROFESSORS & MENTORS

"For every one of us that succeeds, it's because there's somebody there to show you the way out. The light doesn't always necessarily have to be in your family; for me it was teachers and school."

- Oprah Winfrey

Emily's heart pounded against her chest. As she walked to Professor McKinley's desk, she absentmindedly crinkled the letter in her hand.[1]

"Okay... you can do this Emily, just one more step." she thought to herself.

Her walk seemed longer in the moment. Each step gave her a new chance to doubt herself. Finally, her journey ended. She had arrived at the front of the class.

Professor McKinley looked up from his notes expectantly.

---

1   Names, places, and events have been changed in this chapter to protect the identity of the individuals in this story.

Your Relationship GPA

"Does he even remember who I am?" Emily wondered.

Professor McKinley beckoned for her to come closer. "Can I help you?" he questioned. His eyes squinted as if it would help him understand her motivations.

Emily nodded. It was all she could do. Wordlessly, she brought the letter up and placed it on his desk.

The lines of confusion on Professor McKinley's face deepened. He picked up the letter, gently tore off the envelope, and flipped it open.

As he began to read, Emily panicked. "Is that a grimace?" she wondered. "Is he angry?"

But it was too late; his eyes had already begun scrolling across the thank-you note.

LEARNING IS NOT LINEAR

Emily is something of an anomaly at Harvard. She wears flannel, enjoys bandanas, and has a penchant for phrases like "y'all." But since entering college, Emily hasn't paid much attention to how different she might appear. She was too entranced in something else: the playful dance of numbers.

Emily grew up in Little Rock, Arkansas. Since she was a girl, her dream was to become the world's best mathematician. She'd spend nights looking over the theories of her predecessors: from Euclid to Cantor. While Emily was not born a prodigy, she would go on to reach the top of her field through grit and determination.

When Emily was 16, she realized that she couldn't learn enough if she stayed in Arkansas. So, she moved to New York City by herself to continue high school. Over the next two years, Emily kept focusing on her classes. She entered a few mathematics competitions; and though she didn't win, she scored high enough to compete internationally.

In her senior year, Emily applied and was accepted to Harvard College. Harvard's math department is one of the best in the world. Emily was one step closer to fulfilling her dream.

But, when she arrived, she had difficulty talking to professors. She describes it as a problem of identity. "When I was in Arkansas, I never thought, 'man, I am a Southern woman,' I just was. But, when I came to college, I felt isolated. In my sophomore math class, for example, I was the only woman in the entire class."

For her first three semesters, Emily didn't speak to professors outside of lecture. In her sophomore year, her friend approached her with an interesting fact. Of 1600 students in her class, she was one of two female math majors. "At first, I felt proud because I had found my niche. Then I just felt alone."

In her sophomore spring, Emily took Professor Andrew McKinley's class - Algebraic Topology. Andrew McKinley is another rare occurrence in the world of math. He has bushy orange hair, grew up in Louisiana, and is in love with teaching.

During Emily's first class, Professor McKinley stood up at the board. He drew two perpendicular lines - an X-Y axis. He then drew a long line sloping horizontally upwards.

"Most students," he said, "think learning is like this."

He then furiously erased the line. He drew another graph. This time the line spiraled in and out, forwards and backward, and randomly around the board. "But, in reality, learning is like this. In this class, and for the rest of your life, you'll experience moments when you think you know it all. You'll also experience moments when you feel like you know nothing. That means you are doing learning right."

Emily framed the two graphs and hung them in the back of her mind. On the last day of the semester, she decided to thank him with a card.

Professor McKinley's eyes read to the bottom of the paper. Then, he put down the envelope and looked up.

"Emily, what are you doing this summer?"

Emily's southern accent strengthened, as it did when she was nervous, "Uh, well I was planning on taking a summer school class in statistics."

Professor McKinley frowned. "Well, if that's the case nevermind. I was going to suggest you look at the Fibonacci Institute. It's a summer program I help run for women and minority undergraduates interested in math."

Emily gulped. "I, uh, I could probably change my summer school class."

One month later, Emily returned to Harvard to study math. She made lifelong connections, and realized her love for number theory. She calls it the best summer of her life.

The story of Emily demonstrates two truths about college.

First, professors are gatekeepers. They have access to resources, knowledge, and networks that students don't. Professors can change lives.

Second, we can reach professors. Many students complain about professors being "distant." But, as we've discussed, you have to take the initiative. Some professors will handpick students to mentor, but these opportunities are rare. Most professor-student relationships come from a student reaching out. Yet so often, students find reasons to procrastinate connecting with their teachers.

WHY FOCUS ON PROFESSORS?

At first, this question might seem self-evident. Of course you want good relationships with professors. But, as we keep reinforcing, all relationships require trade-offs. Your time is limited. So, the time you focus on an academic is time not spent on friends, family, or your non-existent significant other.

Professors aren't always the easiest to befriend. They're older, they're busy, and they exist in entirely different social circles. You can normally meet friends anywhere: a cafétéria, a library, or a party. But, professors are different. Try inviting your German professor to take tequila shots. You're going to need to go out of your way for these relationships - and therefore you need to understand their value. Emily dreams of a Ph.D. program in math, but if you don't, it can be harder to know what a professor could be in your life.

One opportunity professors can provide is mentorship. In a meta-analysis of 173 studies, Lillian Eby of the University of Georgia investigated the importance of mentorship. For college students, she found that students who received faculty mentorship did better academically, professionally, and psychologically. As she argued, mentors change undergraduates by providing both professional support (introductions to potential jobs, direct-training, etc.) as well as psychosocial support (encouragement, unconditional support, etc.)[2]

As Eby argues, the relationship between professor and student extends far beyond research. Professors serve as sounding boards for students. In an uncertain period of life, an older presence can help undergrads step back and make difficult decisions. As well, by supporting student development, college mentors help students feel a stronger sense of belonging.[3]

College is a period of transition. Growing up, most students have parents or parental figures they rely on. As they

---

2   Eby, Lillian T et al. "Does mentoring matter? A multidisciplinary meta-analysis comparing mentored and non-mentored individuals." Journal of vocational behavior 72.2 (2008): 254-267.
3   Jacobi, Maryann. "Mentoring and undergraduate academic success: A literature review." Review of educational research 61.4 (1991): 505-532.

enter college, their count of older relationships drops. Students have only a few people to provide perspective and advice. Unfortunately, some students leave college without a single connection to a professor. While not all students want or need faculty mentorship, we believe that most would benefit from these once-in-a-lifetime relationships.

College faculty are incredible resources of knowledge, experience, and mentorship. Students need mentors over their time in college and faculty members want to help students grow. For many, it's the reason they became professors. Applying the following steps is not about slickly getting a professor to dinner, it's about breaking down the barrier between you and yet another friend.

Take Initiative: Mastering The (Post-Lecture) Bump And Email

In the book, Never Eat Alone, Keith Ferrazzi describes what he calls the "deep bump." The deep bump involves meeting a person, quickly telling them who you are, what you have in common, and then inviting them to connect later. The key is in creating a brief, but meaningful interaction.[4]

The deep bump is a great way to meet a professor and ask for an outside-class date. Try approaching your professor ten to fifteen minutes after their class. If it is a lecture, wait in the back for other students to talk to the speaker, then, after everyone has

---

4   Ferrazzi, Keith, and Tahl Raz. Never Eat Alone, Expanded and Updated: And Other Secrets to Success, One Relationship at a Time. Crown Business, 2014.

left, approach. Mention something that you found interesting about the lecture or their research, and connect it back to an interest you have. After speaking with them for a couple of minutes, recognize their time constraints, and ask them for a coffee in a couple of weeks. They'll probably give you their email to set-it up later. Send them an email in the next hour giving two or three potential times to meet.

Remember, even if you are not in their class, this is a great way to meet faculty you're interested in. If they teach a larger lecture, email ahead to ask if you can sit-in for one lecture. More often than not, they'll say yes. Introduce yourself afterwards and ask for the outside date. Research on campaigns indicates that face-to-face interactions lead to much higher levels of commitment than online methods such as email or twitter.[5]

MAKE RITUALS: BE AN OFFICE HOUR ADDICT

Have an intellectual crush on a professor? Remember the mere-exposure effect, the more someone sees something, the more they like it. Office hours are your chance to put this into practice - they are times that professors set aside explicitly to talk to students. That means that they're often sitting in their office like a freshman on a Friday night, hoping for someone to come speak with them. Make that someone you.

---

5   Green, Donald P, and Alan S Gerber. Get out the vote: How to increase voter turnout. Brookings Institution Press, 2008.

For your first office hours, start small. Most professors post a syllabus with their availability. In lulls between homework and test deadlines, office hours are often empty. Come prepared with a couple of questions. They might be about the class, the homework, or how to approach a test. Make sure to introduce yourself, your interests, and why you are taking the course.

If you enjoy the conversation, make office hours a regular habit. As we explored in "the rituals" section, relationships are built on repeated time spent together. Eventually, you could create a ritual with your professor outside of office hours. This could be a monthly lunch or a bi-weekly chat. But, in the early stages, make that relationship easy for them by using office hours.

BE VULNERABLE: ASK FOR ADVICE

Once you've exercised the first Cinderella Skill, taking initiative and meeting a professor or mentor in person, what do you say? Bring up an issue related to their expertise and then ask what suggestions they have. For example, if you're taking macroeconomics, ask about a current trend in the news. Professors want to help students, especially when it relates to their area of expertise. By asking for their help, you make them more likely to care for your long term success.

Many people don't ask for advice because they're scared that it will make them look incompetent. However, research from Alison Brooks of Harvard Business School shows the opposite is true. When individuals were asked for advice in their area of specialties, not only did they perceive the asker as more competent, they also liked the person more. By asking someone for advice, you show your respect for their expertise and improve how that someone thinks about you.[6]

Asking for advice is doubly important when meeting professors because you truly do want their help. They're world experts in the field you're studying. As well, they understand your place as a student. They can sometimes give more targeted advice than anyone else in the world.

LISTEN WELL: FOLLOW UP AND FOLLOW THROUGH

The first step in a conversation is always listening. As Harvard University neurologists found, talking about oneself triggers the same brain mechanisms as sex, food, or money. Ask your professors questions and make sure you've understood what they said.[7]

For mentors, however, listening alone is not enough. You must show that you've followed through on their advice. In a study of call center employees, Wharton professor Adam Grant showed that when workers knew how they'd impacted the life of someone else, they performed better at work. For faculty, their

---

6   Brooks, Alison Wood, Francesca Gino, and Maurice E Schweitzer. "Smart people ask for (my) advice: Seeking advice boosts perceptions of competence." Management Science 61.6 (2015): 1421-1435.

7   Tamir, Diana I, and Jason P Mitchell. "Disclosing information about the self is intrinsically rewarding." Proceedings of the National Academy of Sciences 109.21 (2012): 8038-8043.

job is to make a difference in your life. But, it's difficult for them to see progress. By following through with their advice, you show that you genuinely appreciate their opinion.[8]

After listening and implementing a mentor's advice, follow up! Thank them for their time (they are, after all, busy people). Just like Emily did, show your gratitude with a written card. The average U.S. family receives a handwritten letter once every seven weeks.[9] By writing a letter, you'll both stand out and lovingly communicate your appreciation.

GIVE OFTEN: BECOME AN ASSISTANT

At first, helping a professor might feel counterintuitive. What can students give a professor? Shouldn't it be the other way around? Don't fall for this fallacy; everyone needs help in some way or another.

Many professors could use help with their research. If you're interested, this is a great way to become a regular in their life. What's more, your work will cause them to become more invested in your success. Emily began by working with her professor over the summer at the Fibonacci institute. As she grew closer with Professor McKinley, he asked for more of her help. During her junior year he asked her to take over a nationwide initiative he created. She eagerly agreed and each following

---

8   Grant, Adam M et al. "Impact and the art of motivation maintenance: The effects of contact with beneficiaries on persistence behavior." Organizational Behavior and Human Decision Processes 103.1 (2007): 53-67.

9   "2011 USPS Household Diary Study - about USPS." 2012. 5 Jun. 2016 <https://about.usps.com/studying-americans-mail-use/household-diary/2011/fullreport-pdf/usps-hds-fy11.pdf>

month, Emily flew around the United States giving talks about equality in mathematics. Ultimately, Emily met numerous math professors because of her combined project with Professor McKinley; Emily's numerical dreams were coming true thanks to the giving nature of the adults around her.

If you don't like research, you can still give. Some things that are easy for you, such as creating events on campus and reaching other students, might be difficult for a professor. If they're looking for students for a psychology study, offer to help them send an email over an undergraduate email list. If they need help with coding, reach out to your friends studying computer science. As a student, you have access to unique information and networks that faculty don't. So, use them! Your professor will appreciate the help, and your giving will help develop the relationship.

PRIORITIZE: HOW DO YOU PICK THE RIGHT MENTOR?

You have now seen examples of how to take initiative, be vulnerable with, give to, and ritualize your relationships with professors. If all goes well, one of your professors might become a mentor. Someone else could as well - an internship employer, a family friend, or even an older student. Regardless of where they come from, a great mentor is invaluable. They invest in your growth. You invest in their work.

But, as you already know, not all mentors are perfect. Recall your favorite teacher in high school - you might have loved them. But, did everyone in your class feel the same way? It goes without saying that some teacher-student pairs are stronger than others.

To capitalize on a mentor-mentee relationship, you need to choose the right person. Researchers have shown that while positive mentor relationships lead to success, negative mentor relationships can lead to the opposite.[10] In other words, students are better off without a mentor then with a poor one.

So, how do you choose the right mentor? As it turns out, there at least three well-researched factors to consider.

Choosing Mr. Or Mrs. Right

Imagine, you're a freshman walking into your first class. The professor, a jovial, vaguely overweight latino man stands at the front of the room. He calls people in with a loud bellow. His face cracks a broad smile as he starts the class.

You stare at him carefully. "A potential mentor?" you wonder.

Your next class begins more quietly. A tall Chinese woman stands at the front. She asks everyone to write down their name, favorite food, and favorite movie on a slip of paper. She then walks around the class and picks them up.

---

10   Allen, Tammy D et al. "Career benefits associated with mentoring for proteges: a meta-analysis." Journal of applied psychology 89.1 (2004): 127.

You stare at your movie selection - will she think Castaway is cool? Then you look again at the professor. Perhaps she's the one.

Your final class begins with a bang. Literally. The professor stands at a small beaker of smoking liquid. He waves for you to walk in. His curly black hair springs over his safety goggles. He begins to speak, and you immediately notice his voice.

"He's got a great accent," you think. "Is that French?"

In any case, you're sure this time. He's going to be your mentor for the next four years.

When we look for faculty mentors, our decision process can be haphazard. We look for superficial similarities. As Emily described, "It's difficult to reach out to someone who doesn't look like you at all." Unfortunately, this isn't predictive at all of the mentor-mentee success. As multiple researchers have found, there is no relationship between mentoring outcomes and gender, race, or ethnicity.[11]

In the above example, we had three professors who seemed interesting. But, in reality, we had no information to make a decision.

So, if a cute French accent isn't enough, what should college students look for in a mentor? The most important traits are similar core values, a similarity of work interests, and a focus on generosity.

---

11   Allen, Tammy D, and Lillian T Eby. The Blackwell handbook of mentoring: A multiple perspectives approach. Tammy D Allen & Lillian T Eby. Andrew Wiley & Sons, 2011.

TRAIT 1: HAS SIMILAR CORE VALUES

In multiple studies, similarities of attitudes, personalities, and morals predicted mentor-mentee success more than factors like mentor prominence, similarity of fields, or formality of the relationship. Deep-level similarities between the mentor and mentee predicted psychological support, practical support, and relationship quality. Though it was easier to meet mentors of a similar race or gender, surface level commonalities didn't predict a successful relationship.

Mentors want to help students that seem similar to them. As a result, they put in more time, more effort, and take larger risks for these students' success. Take notice of this bias. When looking for a mentor, think first about someone you relate to deeply. No extent of power, connections, or visual similarity can replace that fundamental trait.

TRAIT 2: IS IN YOUR FIELD

If your goal for mentorship is "practical" (i.e. learning, career-related advice, etc.) then you should seek someone with a similar background. As Eby remarked in her meta-analysis of mentorship, "Mentors who are similar to their protégés in terms of educational background, departmental affiliation, or functional area, may be better able to provide appropriate technical guidance, help the protégé engage in networking activities, and recommend the protégé for learning opportunities."

Finding a mentor in your field makes it easier for them to give practical advice. To be clear, this does not mean that mentors outside your area of interest are useless. They can provide emotional support and moral guidance. But, they won't have access to opportunities that more closely related mentors will. Given a choice between two equal mentors in different fields, choose the one in the field you're most passionate about.

Trait 3: Generosity

As we discussed in the "giver" chapter, people have different styles of reciprocity. The same goes for professors. Some will be givers. They enjoy helping students without thought for themselves. Some are matchers. They help out the students who have helped them (or who they particularly like.) Finally, some are takers. They rarely help students. If they do, it's only to advance their own cause.

As Adam Grant explained in his book Give and Take, givers tend to add value to everyone in their network. For you, try to learn the style of giving of each prospective mentor. Ask around. If your mentor is known for their generosity, then seek them out and model yourself after them. If they are known for taking, it's time to move on to someone else.

We often feel powerless when choosing mentors. After all, aren't we lucky to have one? But, as we've discussed, a bad mentor is worse than no mentor at all. You control your relationships, so it's your responsibility to seek out a mentor with these traits.

Before Emily spent a summer at the Fibonacci Institute, she felt trapped by her identity. She didn't reach out to professors and she didn't find her schoolwork interesting. She felt ostracized.

After a summer spent with similar students and faculty, her perspective changed. She realized there were other students like her. More importantly, she became comfortable reaching out to any professor.

Emily had taken the first step with a professor. She showed gratitude in a small written letter. Because of it, her life has benefitted dramatically. She does research during the semester, travels around the U.S. promoting math to women and minorities, and now has multiple role models for her own future. Professors are people too. Reach out, be open, and make sure they know that you care.

PRIORITIZATION

PROFESSORS & MENTORS

DATING

FAMILY & OLD FRIENDS

10
DATING & OTHER REASONS TO COMPLAIN

"We waste time looking for the perfect lover, instead
of creating the perfect love."

- Tom Robbins, American novelist

"You know you can't have them both," Jenny says loudly.

"Exactly," Tim chimes in, "pick one and be happy."

Ah... choice. Your mortal enemy. The combined glare of
your two best friends isn't helping. Sure, you're flirting with both
options. But, how bad is that? The world's not going to end if you
take more time to think.

Jen grabs your hand.

"If you don't make a decision about one of them, then I
will."

You gulp. How could you choose between two loves? And,
perhaps more importantly, how are Jenny's fingers so strong?

Your hand throbs from a strange combination of pain and admiration.

"Okay, I'll make a choice!" you tell her. With that, you hold up the two pictures you've been agonizing over.

The first up is Cherry. Oh man, you like Cherry. Cherry is refined, but not pretentious, sweet, but not too sweet. You could take Cherry anywhere: a concert, a coffee date, even a stay-in night movie. Your gaze softens as you look at Cherry.

Jenny's grip tightens.

You quickly turn to the second picture.

Option two - New York - is the family favorite. And sure, if you'd made the choice out of high school, you'd pick New York. They're from the same hometown, they're the family favorite, and even more they're rich - rich! But, is that all there is to life? Just picking what your family would want?

Your left pinkie begins to lose color.

"Okay, okay. I've decided." You put down the two photographs.

"I'd like the cherry cheesecake," you tell the waiter.

The server, eye now twitching from exasperation, scribbles down your order. His gaze turns to Jenny and Tim, daring them to be original. They decide to have the same.

An awkward silence fills the table. Finally, Tim opens the conversation with a lamenting comment about a hookup.

Last night, he attended a track-team evening social event where he'd enjoyed the free refreshments. Feeling particularly refreshed, he'd approached the crush from his English literature class. One thing led to another, and they "hooked up."

"Hooked up?" you ask. It's a fair question; no one quite knows what the term entails. What did Tim and the girl actually do? Did they kiss? Did they make plans for a date? Did they make like rabbits on Viagra? Regardless of the details, Tim was not in a positive mood.

It turned out the entire hookup had cost Tim six hours of his time - from 8:00 PM to 2:00 AM. He was exhausted, hungover, and morning text messages made it clear that the girl wasn't interested in "anything serious." If only he had a girlfriend, he complains, his life would be complete.

TRYING TO FIND A SIGNIFICANT OTHER

Between sixty and eighty percent of college students report having had some sort of "hook-up" experience in college - yet sixty-three percent of men and eighty-three percent of women said they would prefer a traditional romantic relationship.[1] Why is there a mismatch between desire and reality, and how can you change it for yourself?

Tim's yearning for a relationship has merit. Romantic, steady relationships are an important part of college life. They

---

1   Garcia, Justin R et al. "Sexual hookup culture: A review." Review of General Psychology 16.2 (2012): 161.

provide stability, emotional support, and an excuse to watch The Notebook.

Unfortunately, Tim's desire for a relationship - any relationship - puts him in a dangerous place. His willingness to settle puts him at risk of creating an unsatisfying future.

The student producer of Harvard's premier fashion show, Identities, makes an analogy for settling romantically: "Don't buy a piece of clothing that doesn't fit just because it's on sale. Save up and wait till you find the perfect item. Don't settle for less. The same goes for dating."[2] The early stages of college courtship are emotionally and physically expensive. Don't assume these costs unless you are confident in the person you pursue.

Frugality, however, can be just as bad as settling. Tim would miss every chance at love if he never approached anyone. To beat this trap, he needs to meet people he normally wouldn't - not just the cute girl from lecture. As he interacts with more potential partners, the chance of finding that perfect someone goes up.

So, how do you meet new people? The answer lies in a surprising place: video games, fake guitars, and understanding the difference between a stranger and a friend.

TAKE INITIATIVE: HOW ROCKBAND CAN BE A GREAT WINGMAN

In 2015, Professor Jeff Mogil of Mcgill University wanted to understand why humans feel empathy for some people, but

---

2   Laurie, C. (March 28, 2016) Personal Interview

not others. In particular, he was interested in whether people felt different emotions towards strangers and friends. To research this difference, he decided to do what any rational professor would: he'd ask undergraduates to dip their hands into freezing buckets of water.[3]

In the first condition, Mogil asked undergraduates to come to his lab with a friend. The two participants would enter the lab together. Once inside, he asked the main participant to place their hand into a bucket of cold water for thirty seconds while their friend watched. After the thirty seconds had passed, the participant rated their pain on a scale from one to ten. They then waited a few minutes, presumably to defrost, before the researcher asked both the main participant and also the friend to place their hands into the cold water. Again, they kept their hand in the water for thirty seconds; this time, however, the main participant could see their friend's pained reaction.

In the second condition, Mogil asked undergraduates to come alone to his lab. This time, he paired them with a stranger. Similar to before, the main participant placed their right hand into a bucket of water with the stranger watching. Then, after a small break, both the main participant and the stranger placed their hands into the buckets of water. Again, the participant could watch their partner's expression of discomfort.

---

3   Martin, Loren J et al. "Reducing social stress elicits emotional contagion of pain in mouse and human strangers." Current Biology 25.3 (2015): 326-332.

In each condition, participants put their hand into the same bucket of water. So, they should have felt the same amount of pain - right?

Wrong.

When individuals saw their friends go through the same unpleasant experience, they felt more pain. Empathy receptors led participants to physically feel what their friend was feeling. Even though their hand position hadn't changed, their psychological response had. When we feel close to someone, we catch their emotions.

Interestingly, in the stranger condition, the levels of pain didn't change. The finding perplexed the researchers; what made us empathize with our friends, but seemingly not at all with strangers? When the researchers looked at the post-experiment survey, they discovered one thing was different in the two conditions - the stress levels of the participants.

Imagine, walking into a party full of strangers. If you'd feel a bit of anxiety, that's normal. In fact, it's the response that almost every person would have. When we interact with someone new, our cortisol levels - a stress-related hormone - tend to spike.

Knowing that stress made it difficult for people to empathize with strangers, the researchers asked a follow up question. Could they decrease stress between participants to a friend-like level? In their third condition, researchers again paired a participant with a stranger. But, before they ran the ice-bucket experiment, they asked the participant and the stranger to play "Rock Band" together for fifteen minutes. For those who don't know, Rock Band is a videogame where players use fake instruments to play a song. It's cooperative, fun, and inflates your belief in your music ability.

Amazingly, after only fifteen minutes of playing Rock Band, members of the study showed the same level of empathy with strangers as they did with their college friends. Only a few minutes of interacting decreased the stress response that the original experiment had.

In college, approaching someone you find cute is hard. Not only do you feel stressed about talking to someone new, but they also feel stressed meeting someone they didn't expect. But, the Rock Band experiment should provide hope; if you can get past the first hurdle of talking to someone, becoming comfortable is an incredibly fast process.

There's no secret sauce to approaching people in college. The most effective strategy is to do what Tim simply did; say hi, perhaps tell them your name, and launch into a conversation. If they go to the same school as you, you probably have enough common ground for an early chit-chat. If not, pretty much anything else will do - your favorite music, where you've traveled, what you do for fun, etc. Becoming comfortable is the easy part, you only need to take the first step.

THE DATING GAME

Complaining in a conversation often inspires competition. As you slurp your drink loudly, Jen steps up to the proverbial plate. She's been dating a guy for two years now, since the first weeks of her freshman year. She had what Tim desperately wanted - a committed partner - but like Tim she was unhappy.

Jen feels like her relationship is in a rut. From the outside, they appear to be "madly in love." They both like physics. They have matching pajamas. They even share a Starbucks rewards card. If that's not love, they're not sure what is.

Unfortunately, the relationship hasn't moved anywhere in a while. Sure, they had the "blossoming love stage," in which she would wait, panicked and fidgeting, for his texts. They even had the "comfortable in love stage" in which they spoke openly about bodily functions. Now, they were in the "boring in love stage." The last time they did anything romantic was Valentine's day - which was months ago. She hated the monotony, but she wasn't going to make the first move. That was his job, after all.

BE VULNERABLE: LOVING WITHOUT EXPECTATION

The "whoever cares less wins" mantra permeates college deeper than mono. You might brag to a friend that you started studying for a test the night before. Someone tops you by showing up ten minutes late to the final. Someone tops them by taking the test drunk. Relationships follow the same pattern.

People go to extreme measures to communicate disinterest through text and tone. Even committed couples try not to seem too needy. Unfortunately, this is a vicious cycle: the less interest you show, the less interest you feel in a relationship.

Take the first step in your relationships. If you think someone's cute, talk to them. If you have been going on dates and would like to make things official, be the one to start the conversation. If, like Jen, you are worried about some aspect of a long term relationship, bring it up. Taking initiative in relationships can mean communicating even when it's difficult.

This communication needs to be honest to be beneficial. Sadly, people have a habit of lying when it comes to dating. According to the study "Lying to Get a Date," people are more likely to "deceptively alter their self-presented expressivity and love attitudes to more attractive prospects." Not only were they willing to lie about hazy emotional traits, the participants "reported being more willing to lie about their personal appearance, personality traits, (and) income…. to prospective dates who were higher in facial physical attractiveness."[4] Likewise, on the dating website OKCupid, single men lied about their height by two inches on average. They also lied about their income, raising it by twenty percent.[5] When it comes to love, people seem to be drawn to polishing the truth.

4   Rowatt, Wade C, Michael R Cunningham, and Perri B Druen. "Lying to get a date: The effect of facial physical attractiveness on the willingness to deceive prospective dating partners." Journal of Social and Personal Relationships 16.2 (1999): 209-223.
5   "The Big Lies People Tell In Online Dating - OkTrends - OkCupid." 2010. 5 Jun. 2016 <http://blog.okcupid.com/index.php/the-biggest-lies-in-online-dating/>

Unfortunately, as a relationship progresses, lying becomes more harmful. Lying, even without getting caught, causes members of a relationship to dissociate themselves from their significant other. As psychologist Tim Cole of Dupaul University has found, deception in a relationship is linked to a lack of intimacy. The more you lie, the more you feel disconnected from your partner.

More common than lying is avoiding the whole truth in a relationship. As Cole's study discovered, we fear rejection from a romantic partner more than from anyone else.[6] We avoid uncomfortable subjects because we don't want them to break the peaceful balance we've constructed. We avoid talking about difficult topics because we fear being hurt. However, opening up to your partner rarely weakens the connection; instead, it contributes to a deeper sense of trust.

In the case of, her dating life could benefit from a healthy dose of honesty. If she's feeling bored in the relationship, it's likely that her partner is too. Bringing up insecurities is painful. Who wants to hurt someone they love? However, it's an important step to ensure that both sides are happy.

How do you create spaces for these conversations? You need to invest in times which are uniquely intimate. Though time alone is rare in college, there is one situation when your significant other and you will (almost) always be alone: cuddling.

---

6   Cole, Tim. "Lying to the one you love: The use of deception in romantic relationships." Journal of Social and Personal Relationships 18.1 (2001): 107-129.

Listen Well: How Little Spoon Makes a Big Difference

For years, relationship researchers have known the importance of touch between couples. For example, after holding someone for only ten seconds, your body releases the chemical oxytocin. Oxytocin has been called "the hormone of love;" research has linked it to increased happiness, trust, and pair bonding.

Interestingly, different types of touch elicit different hormonal reactions. Though sex releases hormones like dopamine, serotonin, and oxytocin; more simple forms of contact, like holding hands, spooning, or hugging, is often just as powerful. Researchers in 2014 showed that post-sex touching and talking was a better predictor of marital strength than the amount of sex the couple had.[7] On average, couples spend only fifteen minutes on post-sex cuddling. However, this might not be enough.

If you're intimate with your partner (from kissing to having sex), try spending more time on cuddling. When you're lying in each other's arms, this is the perfect time to ask challenging, meaningful questions. What do we want to be? What do we want from each other? And should we ever become Facebook official?

In college, we're bombarded by outside distractions. So, to listen well in a relationship, create the right opportunities to be

---

7   van Anders, Sari M et al. "Descriptive experiences and sexual vs. nurturant aspects of cuddling between adult romantic partners." Archives of sexual behavior 42.4 (2013): 553-560.

together. Don't relegate cuddling to a "would-be-nice" thing to do, make it a priority every time you're with your S.O.

The Dating Game (Cont.)

Jen looks up from her cheesecake, her story finished. You break the silence with a low murmur of pleasure. You really do love cherry.

As you begin eyeing the menu for a second round of cake, you realize both Jen and Tim are staring at you. You get the feeling it's your turn to be vulnerable about relationship problems. You hate complaining about this sort of thing, but you hate awkward silences even more.

"Here's the thing." you tell them.

You've hit it off with your school's next top model. Thank god you stalked their favorite study spot for a week so that serendipity could work its magic. Your conversations have as much flow and definition as their chiseled body, and you have so much in common. They are even great at texting!

You two made it official last week. But now, you're beginning to panic. You've never kept a hamster alive for more than a month, much less a relationship. You want to make it work, but you don't know what to do. Worse, they just invited you to a concert this weekend, but you have an exam the next day! You don't want to go, but you feel guilty rejecting them in the first week. You look at your friends, pleading for advice.

Make Rituals: Planning For Serendipity

Serendipity may have helped in the early stages of the relationship, but coincidence can't fuel all of your interactions. You can try to spend time with your partner whenever you are "free," but college will batter you with fast-approaching deadlines. If you don't explicitly make time for your better half, you'll quickly find yourself procrastinating them out of your life.

Schedule your steady onto the books. Make it a recurring event. Perhaps every Sunday morning you go out to a fancy brunch. Maybe you don't have classes Thursday mornings, so Wednesdays become pizza and movie night. It's possible you both love The Bachelor. In which case, buy a pint of Ben & Jerry's and snuggle up for a Tuesday night adventure.

Once you make a ritual, protect it from yourself. Strong rituals can grow to symbolically represent the relationship; if you suddenly disrespect one, don't be surprised when your main squeeze takes offense.

Keep in mind not every ritual needs to be with your partner. In fact, some of the best traditions are ones in which you plan to do something for your significant other. Perhaps every Sunday, you spend ten minutes brainstorming ways to show your affection for your partner. In this case, there's one tool to make them feel great: surprise.

GIVE OFTEN: WHY WE SECRETLY LOVE SURPRISES

Have you ever been to a surprise birthday party? If so, think back to the birthday boy/girl's reaction as they opened the door. Perhaps they jumped back in shock. Maybe, their eyes widened in confusion. Likely, they let out a joyfully embarassing scream.

Regardless, they probably felt one thing: pretty darn happy.

In 2015, psychiatry researcher Gregory Berns grew fascinated by the surprise birthday problem. In particular, he was curious how important the "surprise" component was. It was possible that the birthday itself was all that matters, in which case, the surprise would be both unnecessary and time-intensive. However, his intuition said otherwise: was there something special about the unexpected?

Berns decided to measure the neurological reaction to people who received surprises. To begin, he asked participants to enter a Magnetic Resonance Imaging machine known as a MRI. Once inside the MRI, his team used a computer controlled device to squirt fruit juice or water into the mouth of the participant. Sometimes the spritz came in a predictable pattern, and other times the spritz came unexpectedly.[8]

The researchers found that the nucleus accumbens - a part of the brain related to pleasure - was more active when subjects received random squirts. As Berns put it, "the brain finds unexpected pleasures more rewarding that expected ones." And,

---

8   Berns, Gregory S et al. "Predictability modulates human brain response to reward." The journal of neuroscience 21.8 (2001): 2793-2798.

when you think back to a surprise birthday, this probably makes sense. If the birthday boy/girl had known about the event, you'd say that the "surprise was ruined." Likely, this is because there is something desirable about positive shocks.

Students in any stage of a relationship should take note: though performing acts of love is important on special dates (e.g. Valentine's day, birthdays, Christmas, etc.), surprise kindness is even more valuable.

Luckily, college makes these unexpected acts easy to do. If your S.O. (significant other) has an exam, drop them off a care package the day before the test. If you'd planned to watch a movie together, surprise them with a scavenger hunt around campus. If their birthday is in July, host a surprise birthday party in March; they will certainly be surprised. It's the thought that counts - especially if they don't know what you're thinking.

The Dating Game (Cont.)

You finish describing your situation with your budding love interest. Looking around the table at Tim's hopeless pursuit, Jen's growing discontentment, and your own fear of commitment, you realize dating in college is really quite difficult. You thought that your quantum physics final was challenging, but that was multi-dimensional peanuts compared to dating.

You sigh, then look around the restaurant. Perhaps, that second round of cheesecake will make you feel better.

What Dating Is... And Isn't.

Research shows that having a stable relationship can prove a powerful support during the most stressful moments of college. A quality significant other will be there during your lows of college and will celebrate with you during the highs. Quality friends help too, but it is unlikely that even the best of friends will offer physical affection while listening.

On the other hand, having an unstable relationship can be disastrous in college. A majority of your headspace can be consumed by the slightest worry or smallest fight with someone you love. When a relationship ends, your emotional compass can be thrown off for weeks or months. If trouble stirs before a final, good luck giving the exam your fullest attention.

When it's good, it's great. You feel on top of the world and your over-optimistic smile insights murder plots from classmates. When it's bad, it's terrible. You'll stay up late creatively considering how to eliminate joy from the world.

It is not our place to advocate dating, being single, or anything in between. The only type of relationship we recommend is a safe, confident one. While romantic partners are some of the most emotionally charged relationships in college, they're not the only people that need special care. In fact, some of the most precarious relationships are with people who aren't even at school: your family, old friends, and the people you left behind for college.

PRIORITIZATION

PROFESSORS & MENTORS

DATING

FAMILY & OLD FRIENDS

11
RELATIONSHIPS BACK HOME

"You don't have to have anything in common with people you've known since you were five. With old friends, you've got your whole life in common."

- Lyle Lovett

Ah, makeout peak. You're sitting in your Mom's 1994 Toyota Camry. Michael Bublé is playing from your car speakers. You're staring deeply, deeply into the eyes... of your best friend.

"Don't worry," you say, "we'll always be friends."

And yet, as you look out from the hill of your first overly wet kiss, you wonder, "Is that really true? College is only two months away. Will we be friends when we're apart?"

A few months later and your parents are unloading the car on your first day of school. Your dad manhandles a fridge up the stairs. Your mom glares at you. Her eyes shine, wet with a mixture of sadness and ferocity.

"Honey, you will call… won't you?"

"Of course Mom!" You reply, and you mean it. Sure, it's the first day of college. You know school is going to be busy, but of course, you're not going to forget your family. After all, they did get you that lava lamp you asked for. Man, you can't wait for college hangouts by the lava lamp.

Four weeks later and you're sitting on that same couch. It's a Thursday night and your lava lamp illuminates your groovy room. You've finished your work and finally, you're completely, utterly free. College is great.

Then, you feel a small nagging in the back of your mind. Four weeks have passed, and you haven't called your best friend back home once. You've sent texts, and while their messages seem positive, you haven't had a real conversation.

You pick up your phone. As you type in that familiar number, you hear a knock at the door. It's Alex, your roommate.

"Hey sorry, I thought you'd want to know that we're playing cards in the common room - wanna join?"

You look back at your phone. You're conflicted.

Surely, the talk can wait. After all, your high school friend wasn't even expecting a call. You'll call later that night. Plus, you want to get closer to the people in your dorm and this looks like a great opportunity for bonding.

But, you haven't spoken in a month. What happened to "friends forever?" Come on; this is the friend you went skinny dipping with in the neighborhood pond. They helped you through your first breakup. They thought you were cool when you were twelve. Twelve! Surely, they deserve a single call.

How High School Friends Are Different

At every stage of life, we face social limitations. We'd like to be friends with everyone, but we can't. As we mentioned while discussing prioritization, a person can maintain roughly 150 relationships at any one time. As we enter college, we're presented with dozens of new friends. So, unfortunately, some of our high school relationships will inevitably fade.

For most people, this process comes naturally. We enter college, gain new friends, and slowly lose the old ones. In this way, the evolution of friendship is natural. We limit our relationships because we can't handle too many connections at once.

While your priorities may shift, this doesn't imply that your old friends have an adverse impact on your life. Sadly, some people disparage high school friendships. They argue that these connections are born out of convenience. Once you enter college, you find your "true friends."

Unfortunately, separating yourself completely from high school relationships is misguided. It misunderstands the importance of maintaining these friendships.

You share irreplaceable memories with your friends, even if some of those moments you'd like to forget. Your high school friends are central characters in your coming-of-age story. By losing touch with them, you lose touch with parts of yourself.

Logistically, you'll also head home often during your time at college. Many students return home during winter break - if not Thanksgiving - only a few months after school starts. Winter break can last for weeks. Considering that full-time employees receive only an average of two weeks a year of time off, this is a lot. You'll probably spend more time with high school friends than you thought.

Finally, how you treat your high school friends post-graduation sets a bad habit for how you'll treat your college friends post-graduation. If you decide, "I'm in a different place, I don't need to keep in contact with people from high school," then you'll be more likely to make a similar decision after college. If anything, keeping up with high school friends is great practice. It helps you hone the skill of staying in touch with people who matter.

What about family, that other group of loving humans residing back in your hometown? In many ways, there's less risk of losing connection with parents and siblings than with old friends. You could barely talk for your first four years of life, and they still liked you back then.

For better or worse, family will likely stick with you for the rest of your life. Therefore, investing in these relationships pays off long-term. What's more, it's likely that they'd love to reciprocate and remain an active part of your life.

Ultimately, as with all relationships, the choice is yours. Maintaining some high school friendships is important, but keeping them all is unrealistic. Prioritize. Figure out which relationships matter. Then apply the same framework to maintaining them. In this chapter, we'll look at techniques to stay close to family and high school friends, based on the five Cinderella Skills.

Take Initiative: Initiate Contact

"Piglet sidled up to Pooh from behind.

'Pooh!' he whispered.

'Yes, Piglet?'

'Nothing,' said Piglet, taking Pooh's paw. 'I just wanted to be sure of you.'"

These famous lines were written by A. A. Milne, author of Winnie-the-Pooh. They describe Piglet checking in with his best friend for the sake of doing so. Connecting with someone from your past without ulterior motive can be powerful. Think of that special feeling you get when a friend sends you a message that reads, "Hey, just saying hi. Wanted to see how you were doing." Wonderful. Your job is to make everyone feel that way.

Taking the first step with high school friends should be easy. After all, you've been friends for so long! But, after a few months of not talking, you might feel awkward giving them a call. Overcome this feeling and send them a message saying hi. Then set up a time to talk over the phone. Even if it's only fifteen minutes long, your friend will appreciate you taking the first step and reaching out.

In the book Never Eat Alone, Keith Ferrazzi examines how to maintain distant relationships. One of his favorite techniques is called "pinging." Pinging is the art of sending a quick communication to someone to show that you care. This could take the form of a quick text, email or call.[1] Send an inside joke, a video that you like, or something you remembered from high school.

At first, this might feel too formulaic. After all, you're friends. You never needed to "ping" them to stay close. But, recall the earlier narrative. If we aren't intentional with our relationships, we'll lose them. We'll end up focusing on the relationships that are immediate at the cost of the relationships that are most important.

During college, we walk around a lot. Make use of this time. If you have a class that is fifteen minutes away, call a high school friend while walking. Doing so is convenient for you, easy for them, and helps strengthen the relationship. What's more, the conversation ends when you reach your destination, avoiding any chance of it dragging on for too long. If you have a list of

---

1   Ferrazzi, Keith, and Tahl Raz. Never Eat Alone, Expanded and Updated: And Other Secrets to Success, One Relationship at a Time. Crown Business, 2014.

friends from home, keep them in your pocket or on your phone. Make sure you give each of them a call throughout the semester.

Make Rituals: Create A Check-In Time With Family

Claudia Laurie is a Harvard sophomore with a lot of experience with long-distance (family) relationships. She grew up in Sydney, Australia until the age of ten. After that, her family moved to New York for her high school. Throughout it all, Claudia's parents traveled. Her father did work outside of the country. So, for most days, he wasn't home to talk.[2]

At age sixteen, Claudia was a sophomore attending a New York high school. Things were turned upside down when her family approached her with bad news. Because of business, her dad needed to move back to Sydney and her mom was going to start working from Beijing. Claudia faced a choice: stay in New York and finish high school, or move with her parents and begin school anew.

Claudia decided to stay. Doing so meant she was cut off from her parents. While they visited when they could, she found herself living alone for a majority of her time. Despite her choice to live apart, Claudia's family was a core part of her identity and she wasn't willing to let them slip away. As a solution, she crafted a plan to stay in contact. Every other day, she'd call one of her parents. On the off-day, she'd send a quick text to figure out

---

2 Laurie, C. (March 28, 2016) Personal Interview

when the next call would be. In college, Claudia has continued this habit. Every other day, she'll call her Dad. These check-ins range from twenty minutes to an hour. But, no matter what, they happen. They're a time for Claudia to relax and reconnect with a family on the other side of the Earth.

For most students, college is the first time they leave their family. To reliably stay in touch, it's most helpful to create a ritual of connection early on. We form most new habits in the first few weeks of a new environment. So, set out a time to talk with parents or siblings. Perhaps you'll send a video message over breakfast once a week. Or maybe you write them a card once a month. You choose the rhythm. The important part is staying consistent. It will improve the relationship, and it will cut down on time spent worrying.

Be Vulnerable: Open Up About College Life

You'll notice something strange your first break back from college. Your dad offers you a beer. You're invited to "the adult table" for Thanksgiving. Even your grandmother has stopped calling you "honey muffin." You've become an adult in the family.

Congratulations, honey muffin.

This newfound treatment is a key opportunity to change your relationship with your parents. They've given you their trust; now it's your turn to give it back. When they ask about school, don't offer them a canned response about classes.

Instead, let them into your life. You don't need to go into detail about Tequila Tuesday. But, you can open up about drinking, relationships, and difficulties.

In a study of father-child pairs, adult-aged children who had more honest, personal disclosure had closer relationships with their father. In this study, the amount of self-disclosure did not predict interpersonal closeness. Rather, the honesty of the disclosure better predicted success.[3]

The same holds true for friendships. The more honest you can be about college, the better. You and your friends will have different experiences. Some will choose to drink and have sex. Others might not. Some will have close college friends. Others will still be searching for the right group. In either case, the more honest you are, the better for the relationship. The more you hold back, the more you'll feel like your high school friends don't understand your current life.

LISTEN WELL: THE EXCHANGE STUDENT EFFECT

Communication is a two-way street. Don't only self-disclose; be interested in the stories of your friends. You've seen a lot since going to college, and your friends have as well. Their stories are guaranteed to be more interesting than your own, simply because you haven't heard theirs yet.

---

3   Martin, Matthew M, and Carolyn M Anderson. "The father-young adult relationship: Interpersonal motives, self-disclosure, and satisfaction." Communication Quarterly 43.2 (1995): 119-130.

In youth exchange programs, this is called "the exchange student effect." After a year studying abroad, students come back to their hometown ready to share new memories. Want to hear about baguettes? These kids know it all. Interested in Japanese ceramics? "Here, take one," they say. Want to know what kissing a German guy is like? They'll go into uncomfortable detail. They can't wait to talk to their friends about the year they lived away.

As the organizers warn though, don't expect too much interest. Friends might ask a few questions about the traveler's experiences, but they'll soon tire of hearing stories from abroad.

The exchange student effect applies for college students returning home. We all come back with countless stories from school. We all want to share our favorite night at a party. We've all made failed romantic advances. We've all engaged in permanently scarring prank wars and have the therapy bills to prove it.

As Dale Carnegie wrote, "To be interesting, be interested."[4] Indulge your friends. Ask questions about their college hangouts. Enquire about that failed love interest. Listen carefully as they tell you about their worst night so far. In every conversation, let them tell their war stories of college. You'll learn a lot. Plus, they'll enjoy recounting the past months they've had.

---

4   Carnegie, Dale. How to win friends and influence people. Simon and Schuster, 2010.

Give Often: Gratitude & Birthdays

How can you give to people hundreds of miles away? Remember the little stuff. One of the best ways to give is to remember birthdays of friends. Social media makes this easier. But, instead of only commenting online, take the next step. Send a gift, write a letter, or make a quick phone call.

You can also give by bringing people together. When you're back home, plan an event that involves five or more people. It could be an old friend group, or it could be an entirely new collection of individuals. Every time we go back home, our high school social network shrinks. So, the number of large-scale events diminishes.

This decline creates a boring experience. You probably enjoy talking one on one with your best friend, but you don't want every hang-out to be like that. You can make everyone's life more interesting by throwing a party. It might be a dinner party for friends, or perhaps a larger party for a big group. Others will appreciate the opportunity to spend time in a group setting.

Finally, don't forget how unique you are. You go to a different school. So, you have access to ideas and people that other students don't. Ask your friends what they're doing over the summer. If they don't know, help them brainstorm ideas. Opportunities that feel obvious to you will be original to them.

Imagine, you're a student at NYU. You probably have some ideas about internships in New York. To you, these opportunities feel obvious. Your friends talk about them, and your school's administration promotes them. Now, imagine you're speaking with a friend from USC in L.A. They might know about opportunities in California, but they won't know much about New York. You have unique knowledge because of your school. By talking to them about the summer, you'll give them new ideas to explore.

Don't underestimate how much you can do. For the first time, you and your high school friends have access to different information. So, use that information to help them. Ask about their future. Then try to connect them to the right people.

FIVE STEPS TO MAKE GOING HOME AN ADVENTURE

Let's say you follow all of this advice. You have a regular check-in time with friends, you write birthday cards, you even listen (for the fifth time) to that story about the keg stand. But, you still feel stuck. You and your friends sit around reminiscing about the past. It's all you do.

"Remember that one time when…" your friend begins.

"OF COURSE, I REMEMBER THAT ONE TIME," you think. You guys are talking about it for the sixth time now. Your friendship is stuck in the past. You don't know how to get out.

Unfortunately, all old friendships face this turning point. Some friendships stagnate while others continue to grow.

You might feel powerless to change this. But, you can do a lot. If you're intentional about how you spend time back home, you can make sure those friendships continue to develop.

A recent study by Robin Dunbar of Oxford gave evidence to the intuitive idea that the more years you spend away from friends, the smaller and weaker your social network becomes back at home. Furthermore, the longer we spend away from friends, the more our future interactions with them focus on the past.[5]

This isn't necessarily bad: recent research has shown that nostalgia is beneficial for our long-term happiness. But, it's not always sustainable. If each break is simply a dose of high school nostalgia, we'll create a drug with decreasing effectiveness.[6]

It doesn't have to be that way. What if we saw our breaks at home as a time not to "catch-up," but to "move ahead?" Instead of living in the past, we take advantage of the weeks we have to form a new narrative in our friendships. Here are a few ways how.

STEP 1: CREATE ONE RIDICULOUS PROJECT WITH A FRIEND

To be clear, nostalgia in moderate doses is good for you. Research from the University of Southampton shows that

---

5   Dunbar, Robin, and Robin Ian MacDonald Dunbar. Grooming, gossip, and the evolution of language. Harvard University Press, 1998.
6   Wildschut, Tim et al. "Nostalgia: content, triggers, functions." Journal of personality and social psychology 91.5 (2006): 975.

nostalgia helps individuals "feel happier, have higher self-esteem, (and) feel closer to loved ones".[7] However, this research comes with a caveat. For nostalgia to be useful, we need to constantly create new memories.

One way to create new memories is to have one ridiculous project over each break. These can range from filming a video, to throwing a Gatsby-era party at your local Burger King.

Before you arrive back home, talk with one of your best friends and think of a project you want to tackle together. Make it your number one goal for the trip, do it, and add another great memory to the friendship.

Step 2: Reach Out To One New Person:

A number of studies show that there is a positive correlation between the size of your social network and your overall happiness.[8] These findings are great news for someone on their way to college, but it means that being home can be increasingly isolating. One way to counteract this is to reach out to one new person each time you go back.

Now, a "new" person doesn't necessarily need to be a stranger. The beauty of college is that it eliminates historic popularity differences. Ask that "to-cool-for-you" high school

---

7   Routledge, Clay et al. "The past makes the present meaningful: nostalgia as an existential resource." Journal of personality and social psychology 101.3 (2011): 638.

8   Chan, YK, and Rance PL Lee. "Network size, social support and happiness in later life: A comparative study of Beijing and Hong Kong." Journal of Happiness Studies 7.1 (2006): 87-112.

crush to a sophisticated coffee date. Odds are, their impending social isolation will force them to agree.

The other option is to tap into a new network you are a part of. Reach out to alumni of your school, those working in a field you're interested in, or those who are in a similar club.

Adventures are as much about people as they are about the journey. Make new individuals a part of every adventure back home - this can be the surest way to create new experiences.

STEP 3: MAKE A PLAN IN ADVANCE

The key to making home an adventure is to actively shape your time. To be clear, just hanging out at home is not a bad thing. However, if you want to make going home incredible, you have to be proactive with what you decide to do.

A good rule of thumb is to write down your goals for the trip one or two weeks in advance. Writing down your goals helps structure your thoughts and makes them more likely to be achieved.[9] Even more important, however, it gives you time to plan for the events you want to attend or host. Whether you need to purchase a ticket to a show, or invite friends to explore an abandoned house, taking fifteen minutes in advance allows you to make much larger scale plans. The more exciting a project is, the more time it will take beforehand. Give yourself that time: plan in advance your schedule for winter or summer break.

---

9   Matthews, Gail. "Goals Research Summary." Dominican University (2013).

Step 4: Invite A Mentor For Tea

When you go off to college, you also leave behind favorite teachers and coaches. Meet up with someone who changed your life. These people deeply care about you and hearing about your success makes them happy. Undoubtedly, you also care about them and are grateful for everything they've done. Invite them for tea, find them at your old school, or cook them an extravagant mac-and-cheese dinner.

Now that you are older, you have a chance to turn your old heroes into friends. While these examples may not be adventures in the traditional sense, an adventure is simply a way to create memories. Fill these new memories with thanks and appreciation, and you'll brighten the lives of the people who changed yours.

Step 5: Be A Mentor

Do you remember how far away college felt as a high schooler? How much you looked up to the seniors of your high school? Now that you've aged, many students look up to you, what you've done, and who you are. The organizations you led in high school are now run by the kids you knew as sophomores and juniors. Reach out to these groups and offer to plan a dinner or party, or simply ask if anyone would like to meet up to talk about college. Make going home about others and it will be much more fun than making it about yourself.

Seeing friends and family is fun no matter what. But, if we only live in the past, we are doing a disservice to them as well as ourselves. By making each trip a new adventure, we recognize that home is an active and growing part of our life – not something that exists purely in our past.

12

CONCLUSION

"Without a struggle, there can be no progress."

- Frederick Douglass

In 1938, the Grant Study gave sophomore Godfrey Camille a lackluster review.[1]

Physical fitness: "Skinny."

Social skills: "Clumsy at human relations."

Emotional stability: "This boy is turning into a regular psychoneurotic."

As longtime director George Vaillant put it, "Godfrey Camille was a disaster as a young man." Regarding future personal stability, the Grant Study ranked him in the bottom three percent of participants.

Fifty years later, things had changed. Valiant wrote, "by the time he was an old one (Camille) had become a star." His daughter showed "love for her father (that) remains the

[1] Vaillant, George E. Triumphs of experience. Harvard University Press, 2012.

most stunning that I have encountered among (the Grant participants)." At Camille's eightieth birthday, 300 people came to his house for a potluck. At eighty-two, Camille died of a fatal heart attack while climbing in the Alps. His funeral had cars parking in the lawn.

During his service, his son gave a small eulogy, "He lived a very simple life, but it was very rich in relationships." However, if you'd met Camille as a sophomore, you'd never have thought that. If anything, Camille's Relationship GPA would have been terrible. He lacked close friends, confidence to be vulnerable, and the desire to connect with others.

The difference between Camille at a young age and Camille by the end of his life demonstrates that there is always time to change. Doing so requires hard work, commitment, and a dedication to living for others. For Camille, it took a lifetime of effort. For most of us, however, we should try to start as early as possible. As we'll show with an example from Oxford, the sooner you start practicing the Cinderella Skills, the better your relationships will be.

Compounding Opportunity And Your Zodiac Sign

In 2013, the BBC set out to understand the core characteristics of Oxford students. What led a student in England to be accepted to one of the most elite schools on earth? Was it their educational background? Socio-economic status? Or could it be an inherent ability such as "grit?"

As the report found, all of these factors mattered. But to much surprise, one of the most predictive components was something rather unscientific: a participant's Zodiac sign.

In 2013, Oxford accepted thirty percent more Libras than Leos, twenty percent more Scorpios than Cancers, and seventeen percent more Sagittarii than Geminis. If a Leo looked at her horoscope the day after applying to Oxford, the prediction might fittingly read, "you will face unexpected difficulty this year."[2]

At first, the researchers were confused; why would Zodiac signs predict college admissions? Sure, everyone knows that Libras display "deep wisdom" and "internal strength." But, even then, ambiguous fortunes couldn't account for such a significant discrepancy.

As the BBC dove deeper into the results, they realized that this effect wasn't unique to Oxford. In fact, if you look at most prestigious universities on earth, students seem to congregate around certain zodiac signs. After exploring the results, the researchers realized that it wasn't someone's zodiac sign that mattered, but rather their date of birth. Students born in certain months were more likely to attend Oxford than others. In fact, students born in the autumn months of September, October, and November (Libra, Scorpio, and Sagittarius) were roughly twenty-

---

2   "Month of birth affects chance of attending Oxbridge - BBC News." 2013. 5 Jun. 2016 <http://www.bbc.co.uk/news/uk-politics-21579484>

five percent more likely than students born in summer months (Leo, Cancer, and Gemini).

But, why would date of birth affect admission rate? And why would September be so much better than August?

In British public schools, the cut-off for the public school year occurs on the 1st of September. Students who are born on September 1 are therefore placed in the same grade as students born a year later on August 31. In the eyes of the school, these students are the same age. But, biologically they're not. Student born on September 1 have had an extra year to grow both physically and mentally.

Unfortunately, it's difficult for teachers to discern between natural ability and age in a classroom. So, when teachers speak with students born in the fall, they naturally appear to be more mature than their younger peers.

At first, this shouldn't matter. But, as research has shown, students meet the expectations they are given. English teachers perceive students born in September and October to be more intelligent. Therefore they give them more challenging assignments and more personalized attention.

Over time, the different treatments between the two groups accumulate. Students who are born earlier in the year are pushed harder. For example, these students are more likely to enter gifted education programs. They grow faster and perform better in school. This early success then leads to more opportunities. These opportunities, again, push these students to learn more, widening the gap. Researchers call this "a virtuous cycle;" students who do well initially have more chances to learn long-term. Over time, they do better.

This phenomenon is called "the relative age effect" and it persists everywhere. For Canadian hockey players, MLB baseball players, and international soccer players, the age cut-off is January 1. Unsurprisingly, the majority of players are born in the early months of January, February, or March. In almost every skill - from mathematics to motocross - early success compounds towards future success.[3]

We believe there is a similar effect for your Cinderella Skills. College is the first time we enter the world as social adults. For many of us, it's around the age we become sexually active, drink, and hold our first job. While social situations vary dramatically throughout childhood, college is an entrance into the adult world. From there, most relationships remain relatively similar. The types of conversations you have in college reflect the kinds of conversations you'll have when you're fifty. The social skills we develop now can last for the rest of your life.

The other tenet of "the relative age effect" is compounding opportunity. In the case of academics and sports, the date of birth itself didn't matter. Instead, the early advantage led to more opportunities for practice. As students performed well, the school tracked them into more challenging classes. Given time, extensive practice resulted in a non-age related difference in skill.

---

3   Musch, Jochen, and Simon Grondin. "Unequal competition as an impediment to personal development: A review of the relative age effect in sport." Developmental review 21.2 (2001): 147-167.

The same holds true for your Cinderella Skills. The better you connect with others, the more time others will want to spend with you. As you improve your social skills, you gain more opportunities to practice. Again, a virtuous cycle of improvement results.

Unfortunately, Camille did not benefit from the zodiac effect. He was not born with the gift of gab, nor did he always possess an inner desire to reach out to others. Luckily, Camille got a second chance in the strangest of circumstances. As his health began to fail, his relationships finally started to bloom.

MAKING THE CHANGE

At the age of 6, Camille climbed a cherry tree to look for blossoms. As he moved up to the top branch, his fingers began to slip. Unable to catch himself, Camille fell twelve feet to the ground.

When his father saw him fall, he said nothing. The man walked silently to his crying boy, picked him up, and then spanked him for disobeying an order not to climb the tree. As Camille explained looking back, "I neither liked nor respected my parents." Thirty years later a child psychiatrist reviewed Camille's file. He declared it one of the bleakest childhoods he had ever seen.

College didn't treat Camille much better. There he was lonely and spent most of his time in the college infirmary.

Outside of the infirmary, Camille coped by complaining loudly to his classmates.

When the Grant Study men entered their early twenties, World War II broke out. Again, the Harvard study found an opportunity to measure "success." The best men, they presumed, would climb the military ladder quickly. The worst would remain at lower ranks.

Unsurprisingly, Camille achieved little compared to those around him. After a few years of service, Camille returned as a private. Other Grant participants had gained the rank of lieutenant or captain during their years.

After Camille left the military, he entered medical school. Upon graduating, he again had difficulty connecting with patients. As we discussed in Chapter 2, empathy is a crucial predictor of successful doctors. For Camille, this felt impossible. Whenever he opened up, he felt his patients' problems add on to his own. As a result, he closed himself off from others.

After a few years as a doctor, Camille felt desperately alone. His life reached a low point with few friends, family, or feeling of belonging. In desperation, Camille attempted to commit suicide. Luckily, he failed.

At the age of thirty-five, Camille contracted pulmonary tuberculosis. For the next fourteen months, his doctor ordered bed rest in a hospital. He could not leave. Instead, he read and spent time with the nurses who cared for him. When he finally left the hospital, he looked like a changed man.

"Camille felt his time in the hospital was almost like a religious rebirth," described Vaillant.[4] Indeed, it was during this brush with death that he began to focus on his Cinderella Skills. As Camille sat in the hospital bed, he'd made a promise to himself; he'd focus on others before himself, even if it cost him his life.

And as Camille began to prioritize others, his life took a positive turn. Released from the hospital, Dr. Camille became an independent physician, met a woman he'd eventually marry, and grew into a responsible father. At the age of forty-five, ten years after his hospitalization, he began to direct his own clinic. Perhaps owing to his own bleak upbringing, Camille had a special talent for listening to patients with troubled childhoods. Soon, he was writing papers about how to connect with patients - a sharp contrast from his college-age self.

And, as he grew older, his Cinderella Skills grew with him. He returned to the church where he took initiative by creating community events for friends and family. After a divorce, he continued exploring new relationships. Whereas relational setbacks had devastated him in the past, this time he pushed forward to meet new people. By the time he was seventy-seven, he had a new love, tended a flourishing garden, and could play squash with men thirty years his younger.

Camille's life illustrates two important messages. First, focusing on your Relationship GPA and your Cinderella Skills is a lifelong activity. While your academic GPA ends in your fourth

---

4   Vaillant, George E. Triumphs of experience. Harvard University Press, 2012.

year of college, your relationships don't. As Camille shows, you should never give up investing in others.

Second, you can start compounding your abilities at anytime. If taking initiative, listening well, being vulnerable, making rituals, and giving often don't come naturally to you, don't be discouraged. As the zodiac effect shows, no one is born an expert. We only get there through concerted practice.

Wherever you're heading, whoever you are, however old you are, you can always reorient yourself. Relationship skills are an investment; the sooner you start investing, the better off you'll be. Camille started in his forties. You can start now.

ACKNOWLEDGEMENTS

We are blessed to have friends, family, and mentors with extraordinarily high Relationship GPAs. To begin, we're deeply indebted to the seven students profiled in this book. Thank you, Nina Hooper, Taylor Carol, Morgan Breitmeyer, Ana Olano, Claudia Laurie, Neil Alacha, and Ben Blumstein. You represent the best the world has to offer; you're smart, driven, and utterly compassionate to those around you.

A cohort of people put in dozens of hours into the book. Christina Foster, Kathryn Turban, Claudia Laurie, and Daniel Turban, thank you for reading through the entire book and giving at times intensely snarky comments. Zoë Burgard, in particular, deserves commendation. During her final year of college, she served as a de facto editor, publicist, and matron saint of the book. Thank you so much for guiding us in the process.

We owe a special thanks to Tom Dingman for his foreword and for the example he sets at college. As any student would agree, Dean Dingman represents the best of Harvard: he's fiercely loyal, caring, and committed to creating the best freshman experience in the world. David Meerman Scott similarly served as both a source of inspiration and a needed reality check for the book. We wouldn't have begun on this adventure without his example.

In the words of Socrates, "It takes a village to build a Rome." So, for loving us despite the thousands of mistakes, mess-ups, and jerk-moves we've made, we'd like to thank our families. In particular, we'd like to thank our parents for reading so much to us as children. Without their countless hours, and brazen mispronunciations of words like "Hermione," "Hagrid," and "Accio," we would never have had the misplaced confidence to begin this endeavor.

We'd also like to thank those who read and gave feedback to early chapters. Thank you, Michael Johnston, Benjamin Betik, Tomas Reimers, Kendall Burchard, Gus Mayopoulos, Leigh Anne Foster, Patricia White, Kelsey Harper, Ronia Hurwitz, Yehong Zhu, Rana Bansal, Noah Yonack, Michael Richard, Michael Bervell, Barbara Lewis, Sheila Rendl, Suzanne Renna, and Karen Kennedy for your insightful comments!

As much as we've taken from social science, we've learned even more from the remarkable people and organizations around us. Though there are too many to list, people like Hajar El-Fatihi, Jarrod Wetzel-Brown, and David Garvin inspire us every day with their valedictorian-like Relationship GPAs. Similarly, organizations like the Franklin Fellowship and Room 13 remind us that even at a pressure-cooker like Harvard, intentional communities can help vulnerability triumph over fear.

Like all institutions, Harvard has flaws. But, in our short time here, we've found a community of people truly dedicated to others. We would not have written this book, become friends, or even met had it not been for Harvard (and Kimberlyn Leary's freshman seminar), thank you.

Collaboration is always an epic journey, and this was no different. From writing drunk in Reno, Nevada to chugging Soylent in San Francisco, writing together was one of the peaks of our college years. We couldn't imagine doing it with anyone else.

APPENDIX

36 Questions To Fall In Love[1]

Developed by Arthur Aron, Edward Melinat, Elaine N. Aron,
Robert Darrin Vallon, and Renee J. Bator

Set I

1. Given the choice of anyone in the world, whom would you want as a dinner guest?

2. Would you like to be famous? In what way?

3. Before making a telephone call, do you ever rehearse what you are going to say? Why?

4. What would constitute a "perfect" day for you?

5. When did you last sing to yourself? To someone else?

6. If you were able to live to the age of 90 and retain either the mind or body of a 30-year-old for the last 60 years of your life, which would you want?

7. Do you have a secret hunch about how you will die?

8. Name three things you and your partner appear to have in common.

---

1 Aron, Arthur et al. "The experimental generation of interpersonal closeness: A procedure and some preliminary findings." Personality and Social Psychology Bulletin 23.4 (1997): 363-377.

9. For what in your life do you feel most grateful?

10. If you could change anything about the way you were raised, what would it be?

11. Take four minutes and tell your partner your life story in as much detail as possible.

12. If you could wake up tomorrow having gained any one quality or ability, what would it be?

Set II

13. If a crystal ball could tell you the truth about yourself, your life, the future or anything else, what would you want to know?

14. Is there something that you've dreamed of doing for a long time? Why haven't you done it?

15. What is the greatest accomplishment of your life?

16. What do you value most in a friendship?

17. What is your most treasured memory?

18. What is your most terrible memory?

19. If you knew that in one year you would die suddenly, would you change anything about the way you are now living? Why?

20. What does friendship mean to you?

21. What roles do love and affection play in your life?

22. Alternate sharing something you consider a positive characteristic of your partner. Share a total of five items.

23. How close and warm is your family? Do you feel your childhood was happier than most other people's?

24. How do you feel about your relationship with your mother?

Set III

25. Make three true "we" statements each. For instance, "We are both in this room feeling ... "

26. Complete this sentence: "I wish I had someone with whom I could share ... "

27. If you were going to become a close friend with your partner, please share what would be important for him or her to know.

28. Tell your partner what you like about them; be very honest this time, saying things that you might not say to someone you've just met.

29. Share with your partner an embarrassing moment in your life.

30. When did you last cry in front of another person? By yourself?

31. Tell your partner something that you like about them already.

32. What, if anything, is too serious to be joked about?

33. If you were to die this evening with no opportunity to communicate with anyone, what would you most regret not having told someone? Why haven't you told them yet?

34. Your house, containing everything you own, catches fire. After saving your loved ones and pets, you have time to safely make a final dash to save any one item. What would it be? Why?

35. Of all the people in your family, whose death would you find most disturbing? Why?

36. Share a personal problem and ask your partner's advice on how he or she might handle it. Also, ask your partner to reflect back to you how you seem to be feeling about the problem you have chosen.

Made in the USA
Middletown, DE
14 July 2016